MASTERING
YOUR
G.A.P.

MASTERING
YOUR
G.A.P.

UNLOCKING THE LEADERSHIP POWER OF
GRAVITAS, AWARENESS, AND PRESENCE

JACOB WERKSMAN, DBA

Worth®

Published by Worth Books
Distributed by Simon and Schuster

Library of Congress Control Number: 2025901778

Print ISBN: 978-1-63763-429-5
E-book ISBN: 978-1-63763-430-1

Cover Design by Rebekah Vasquez
Jacket Design by Bruce Gore
Interior Design by Bill Kersey

Dedicated to the curious,
the committed,
and the courageous.

CONTENTS

Introduction 13

Chapter 1: The Data Behind GAP 23

Chapter 2: Gravitas 47

Credibility Can Be a Liability 48
    Scott Campbell, USAF Colonel and TOPGUN Fighter Pilot Instructor

Ready or Not, You're CEO. 53
    Jerry Morgan, CEO and Board Member of Texas Roadhouse Inc.

Briefing the Admiral 58
    Jason Lamb, US Air Force Intelligence Officer of the Year

"50 Percent of My Time in The Boardroom Was GAP" 64
    Diana Markaki-Bartholdi, Founder and CEO of The Boardroom

Monkey Work 69
    Ted DeZabala, Chief Strategy, Innovation, and
    Technology Officer at Deloitte

A Sale Gone Wrong 74
    Joe Nunziata, Cofounder and CEO of FBC Mortgage, an Acrisure Company

"We're Moving the Company Headquarters" .78
    Rabbi Rob Thomas, Founder and CEO of Team Cymru

A Speech That Changed My Life 85
    Admiral William H. McRaven (US Navy, Retired)

Leading as the Youngest in the Room 94
    Rod Fox, Founder and CEO of TigerRisk Partners

Chapter 3: Awareness 101

"Oh Shit, I Was Promoted—Oh Shit, I Might Be Fired" 102
Robert Schleusner, Head of Wholesale Credit at Bank of America

Soviet Counterintelligence Meets the Beauty Industry 109
Jennifer Walsh, Founder of Beauty Bar

Time-Sensitive Transformation 114
Chris Brown, USA Women's Olympic Rugby Team Head Coach

Shattering My Perfect World 119
Jeff Boyer, Vice President of Global Vehicle Safety at GM

When You Become Aware, Act! 125
*Lauren Crandall, Three-Time Team USA Field
Hockey Olympian and Team Captain*

Awareness for Survival 130
Jessica Buchanan, Humanitarian and Hostage Rescued by SEAL Team Six

Forging Two Cultures to Cultivate Performance 135
Iván López, Global President of Financial and Assistance Services at Assurant

The Sometimes Seriousness of Music 139
*Simon Katz, Vice President of Artists and Repertoire
at A Top Record Label Company*

Chapter 4: Presence 147

"And Just like That, I Was No Longer CEO" .148
Justin Delaney, Serial Entrepreneur of Well-Known Companies

Be Bold—For Yourself and Your Team. 153
*Samantha Weeks, Chief Transformation Officer at Shift4
and USAF's First Female Solo Thunderbird Pilot*

Compromises Sabotage Your Potential 159
Joe De Sena, Founder and CEO of Spartan Race

Going Global with a Performance Management System. 164
*Gabrielle Ivey, VP of Learning and Organizational
Development at Cracker Barrel*

The Perfect Storm. 170
  Chris Rubio, COO at William P. Clements Jr. University
  Hospital at UT Southwestern Medical Center

Chapter 5: Balancing GAP: Gravitas, Awareness, and Presence. 175
My Thirty-Minute Meeting with Bob Iger. 177
  Dan Cockerell, Vice President of the Magic
  Kingdom, Walt Disney World, Florida
The Day I Walked Out of the Executive Team Meeting 185
  Anne Marie Jess Hansen, CEO of Copenhagen
  Business School Executive Foundation
Growing Up in the Projects 191
  Christopher Brown, COO of North America's
  Talent Solutions Solutions at Aon
Three Bad Days in Thirty Years. 198
  Jon Cute, Orlando Police Department SWAT Officer
"I Ran Myself into the Ground" 204
  General Robin Rand (US Air Force, Retired)
First Waco, Now This? 211
  Gary Noesner, Chief of the FBI's Crisis Negotiation
  Unit and Hostage Negotiator
Becoming Partner at McKinsey in Five Years 216
  Bill O'Keefe, Partner at McKinsey and Company

Chapter 6: The Playbook. 227

Acknowledgments 243
About the Author. 245
Notes 247

PART 1

UNDERSTANDING GAP

INTRODUCTION

*F*or four years, my coaching client James had been an emerging leader with high potential at McKinsey and Company—one of the top management consulting firms in the world—at the New York office, where he had been working since finishing his MBA at Harvard Business School, and he was on track to become a partner. As James was heading into the office early one fall morning, he got a call from the managing partner, Leo, who asked if James would meet him for lunch at the firm's club. Of course, James said yes. He couldn't help but think it was his moment. He was sure Leo was going to tell James that the firm would like to offer him the prestigious title of partner in the firm.

James and Leo ordered iced teas in the club overlooking the New York City skyline. Leo began the conversation by sharing how impressed he and the other partners had been with James's performance over the last five years. James thought, *This is it. Say it Leo, tell me I am being made partner.* But Leo's voice changed and he said, "I'm just going to cut to it. You are not being made partner, and unless you change, I don't see you ever being a partner here."

James's heart raced, his appetite was lost, and confusion swirled through his head. Apparently, James didn't do a good job of concealing his confusion. Leo looked James in the eyes and said, "You just don't have the *gravitas, awareness, and presence* required to be a partner."

Have you ever been in this position or something similar before?

Ever questioned how others receive you when you meet for the first time?

Ever met someone and said to yourself, *I don't know what it is about them, but I want to be around them more; they have great energy.*

Ever wondered if you have what it takes to get to the next level?

If you answered yes to any of the above, you're in good company. If you didn't answer yes but you are curious to learn more, you came to the right place.

The scientific research and real-world case studies show that the key to getting to the next level can often be associated with your ability to master what I call your GAP: *gravitas, awareness,* and *presence.*

I have had the honor and pleasure to work alongside thousands of global executives and emerging leaders in my private coaching practice, Victory Strategies, and through my work as an executive leadership coach at Harvard Business School, guiding those who come to Boston to gain a competitive advantage, reach the next level, and embrace the possible.

Do you know what the number one area of identified development is among these high performers? Their desire to learn, adapt, and implement methodologies to master their GAP.

My coaching client James would go on to make partner two years from that intense conversation with Leo. During our coaching sessions together, we got tactical with the frameworks and methodologies—shared in this book—that would help him enhance and ultimately master his GAP and gain the *gravitas, awareness,* and *presence* he needed to get where he wanted to be.

In this book, we'll dig into what each of these key elements means.

Gravitas is the influence, emotions, and feelings someone's demeanor evokes in others.

My concept of **awareness** is composed of four types of awareness, what I like to call SA4:

- Self-Awareness: The perception of self being aligned with the perception of others

- Situational Awareness: Understanding the context and details of an event or action
- Social Awareness: Understanding of the context and details of an exchange between two or more people, often determined by the environment
- Sensory Awareness: The sensory responses (emotion, voice changes, body position, eye contact, etc.) to a situation or event

Presence is your state of being—in mental, emotional, social, and charismatic forms.

In the coming case studies, we'll explore how gravitas, awareness, and presence are interdependent. They amplify each other, and if someone is lacking in one of the three, chances are, the other two are suffering.

So we seek to develop them in perfect balance. Here is an illustration of what I mean:

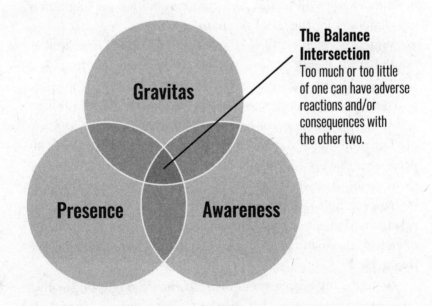

What happens if we veer outside the balance intersection? If we have too much of one, not enough of another? Another client comes to mind to illustrate this situation. My client was the chief operating officer for an international drug store chain. He scheduled weekly team meetings with his direct reports, but these meetings became standard operating procedure, and with that came some complacency and weakening of his awareness. While his position and demeanor instilled strong gravitas (his effect on others) and his attention to his meeting's agenda and time-management demanded his presence (his ability to react to his situation and colleagues in real time), he fell short in his awareness. This resulted in him not picking up on signs from his direct reports that they needed more from him. He was creating an environment where they didn't feel like they could ask for his support and assistance with some obstacles they were facing inside the company. In our coaching, we identified this through some peer feedback tools. We built up his awareness through specific methodologies and techniques to get him in a more balanced state. This resulted in an increase in his team's performance abilities, making him a top contender for the CEO position.

Whichever element of GAP you hope to work on first, keep in mind that the balance is key. And so is continued growth.

Those I work with often fall victim to the common misconception that once they receive positive feedback on their GAP through a 360-degree evaluation or peer feedback, they can check the box of "I'm good here." But really, GAP never reaches a peak of 100 percent satisfaction. It's similar to your integrity; just because you prove to be trustworthy once doesn't mean you never have to be trustworthy again. Mastering your GAP requires continuous practice and intentionality. Through consistent growth, my clients often have the ability to get slightly better at each component every single day.

So, once my clients strengthen up each element of gravitas, awareness, and presence, how do they continuously enhance their mastery? Through what I call the GAP Enhancement Cycle. Let's dive in below.

GAP Enhancement Cycle

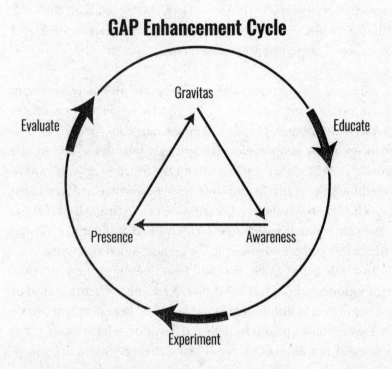

The GAP Enhancement Cycle continuously progresses from *educate* to *experiment* to *evaluate*, ensuring that you benefit from every learning repetition and experience.

In the **educate** phase of the cycle, you come to thoroughly understand what GAP is and how to build it. This is what you'll experience in the first two parts of this book.

When you **experiment,** you put that knowledge and understanding into action as a practitioner.

And finally **evaluate** is to debrief and reflect on what went well and what could have gone better in the experiment phase. You'll find tools for both *experiment* and *evaluate* in the final part of this book.

When the educate, experiment, evaluate circle is put into action, you can continuously cycle through the phases for ongoing development and growth of your GAP, increasing your GAP through every complete rotation. The good news about the GAP Enhancement Cycle is that it is entirely within your control, and you choose how to apply each element.

Gravitas, awareness, and presence are not new concepts. Thousands of years ago, Lao Tzu said, "He who conquers others has physical strength. He who conquers himself is strong."[1] GAP is a concept many people reference and may talk about but few can actually define; yet, as you'll learn, it is statistically proven to have incredible value for individual and team performance. If my client James had been a conscious practitioner of increasing his GAP, his initial conversation with Leo could have had a different outcome and not delayed his partnership for an additional two years.

In reading this book, you will have the opportunity to thoroughly understand what GAP is and examine scientific studies and research that emphasize its value. You'll hear personal stories from some of the greatest leaders in the world—who at times either did or did not have GAP—and learn their personal takeaways on enhancing your GAP. Finally, scientific action resources are provided to assist you in mastering your GAP. My inspiration for creating this book was to equip you with the knowledge, practical guidance, and scientifically tested tools to accelerate your leadership and performance abilities by mastering your GAP.

WHAT GAP MEANS TO ME

What you are about to read comes from a lifetime of experience—not just in leadership and executive coaching and research but, for me, from the very beginning of my story. I've always been curious about what contributed to other's success, both macro and micro components. From childhood, I believed in the American dream: that with the right mindset and determination, we can build a good life for ourselves and our families. I learned this from my parents. They met on a kibbutz in Israel. My father, originally from Massachusetts, had moved there to live. My mother was from Denmark and had volunteered to work at the kibbutz. Once they decided to get married, they moved to the United States with only a few hundred dollars, plus love and ambition. My mother went to nursing school and my dad started a company selling office furniture.

One afternoon, while running errands, my dad mentioned that he had served in the Israeli Defense Forces. I was shocked. I had lived my entire eight years never knowing that he was a soldier. I barraged him with questions: *Where did you go? Have you shot a gun? Have you killed people?* This was the beginning of my interest in joining the military.

I was a little "husky," as my father called it, when I was a kid. Then, in eighth grade, I lost weight, got into shape, and made healthy eating a priority. But that "husky" feeling never left me, and I always pushed back against people who mocked other people's appearances. I associated the targeted individuals' feelings with my own. Meanwhile, I joined the football, lacrosse, and swim teams at school. I was an average student academically, not quite sure where I might go to college. I didn't really have a plan until the summer between my sophomore and junior year of high school.

It was a comfortable summer night with clear skies and stars. I was sitting around a fire with my friends. "I want to be a part of a team that has a stronger bond than our football team," I said. "I want to go into the military."

The next day I began researching possible places to enlist. By my senior year, I knew I wanted to be a Navy SEAL. My parents supported me in this, and instead of going to a nonmilitary college, I joined the navy's Basic Underwater Demolition/SEAL training program. It was one of the most rewarding experiences I could imagine. I was surrounded by men from all walks of life. The training pushed me to limits that I didn't know were achievable by the human body. I became a US Navy SEAL in August 2014, went to sniper school, and ultimately was deployed in eleven countries in Western and Eastern Europe, plus Israel.

Though I didn't plan it that way, the military exposed me to a profound understanding of the elements that would become GAP. It started right at the beginning, and a lack of it almost cost me my career as a Navy SEAL.

It all started during Basic Underwater Demolition/SEAL (BUD/S) training, which has three critical selection phases, lasting roughly two months each. The first phase is the most notorious; it features Hell Week, an intense five-and-a-half days where students get no sleep; run more than 250 miles with a rubber boat on their head; and are cold, wet, and sandy the entire time. The second phase is dive training, where students are introduced to open- and closed-circuit diving equipment and learn to be tactical in the water. The third phase is weapons and demolition training. The bulk of training takes place off the coast of California.

My transformative moment, what I like to call the "peanut butter and jelly incident," happened halfway through that last weapons and demolition phase. After every day's training, our class of forty-four students had a long list of collateral duties. These were chores like washing and vacuuming the vehicles, cleaning our weapons, and sweeping the classroom floors. We typically wouldn't finish them until midnight. At that point, we could either regroup in the chow hall and eat peanut butter and jelly sandwiches or gain an extra thirty minutes of sleep. This was not an easy choice.

Believe it or not, I valued sleep over the sandwich. Every night, when we finished our collaterals, I went to my room, worked on my gear, and got into bed. My classmates stayed up an hour later in the chow hall, talking and telling jokes as they ate. They would return to find me already asleep in my rack.

Then came one of our biweekly peer evaluation days, where we ranked and rated our fellow classmates on performance, attitude, commitment to team, and trust. When the rankings were posted, with just two weeks left to go, I was surprised to see my name had fallen from the middle to the bottom five. Nobody wanted to be in the bottom five. The instructors saw that group as problem cases who would need extra attention to make it through. Some people had been cut from the program after being slotted that low.

So I asked some classmates for verbal feedback. Why had they pushed me down the ranks? They all gave me the same response: "You're the first one in your rack every night, sleeping." They mistakenly perceived me as slacking on my collateral duties.

Without hesitation, I changed my pattern. Rather than trying to convince my classmates that I was doing my fair share of collaterals, I joined the group for sandwiches every evening. On the final peer evaluation, I was happy to see my name back in the middle of the rankings.

I learned from that episode that I lacked a key element of GAP: awareness, specifically self-awareness. I did not realize that others perceived me and my actions differently from the way I did. The experience immediately humbled me. From then on, I prioritized not just self-improvement but visible improvement—starting with awareness and incorporating elements of presence and gravitas as I learned about them.

At the peak of my SEAL career, I held the title of Reconnaissance Team and Sniper Team Leader, managing up to fifty-four Navy SEALs during certain cycles of my military career. I went from there to business and management, which took me from being an expert in my craft back to being a beginner. This is where GAP came into play yet again. I had enough self-awareness by now to identify where I was confident and competent and where I needed to learn.

I'd attended the University of Charleston in West Virginia while I was active duty in the military, earning a degree in organizational leadership. But I knew I needed to learn more about the specifics of business and leading in the commercial sector. So

I went from there to Harvard Business School for their executive MBA alternative, called the Program for Leadership Development. Around the time I transitioned out of the military, I created a leadership assessment, training, and coaching company, Victory Strategies. This was where the concept of GAP began to take form.

My first book, *Leadership a Life Sport,* tells this story in more detail, with an emphasis on the attitudes and disciplines I learned as a SEAL. The book fed into my coaching practice, and I learned that many other people had been through similar life-changing experiences. At Harvard's Executive Education Programs, most of the career executives I coach have similar preoccupations. When asked about their life goals, they nearly always mentioned gravitas, awareness, or presence. They don't care so much about what they *did.* They care about who they *are* and how others perceived them.

So, I began researching. I focused entirely on leadership, gravitas, awareness, and presence. I found some links between self-awareness and emotional intelligence, and a great deal of illuminating anecdotal evidence. Rather than publish these findings in academic papers only, I chose to write a book for real-world leaders and managers—for you—bringing research and practice together. That brings us to where we are today. You are about to read the highlights of that research and the findings that underscore the importance of GAP in the real world. Then, you'll find a collection of interviews and case studies from remarkable individuals who illustrate the importance, successes, and failures of GAP in action or not in action. Then I will share the coaching tools and methods that crystalized from my exploration of GAP—in ways that you can apply directly to your life, today. But first, let's engage in the *educate* phase of what I came to call the GAP Enhancement Cycle—to build your base of knowledge as a personal foundation for success.

CHAPTER 1

THE DATA BEHIND GAP

*I*n the course of my work, I've met some fascinating and remarkably successful individuals. I've encountered them in my philanthropic work with military special operations, with Olympic athletes transitioning from those professions and retiring into the commercial sector, and when I coach entrepreneurs facing the sale of the company they founded and who need to define what the next chapter looks like for them. Without a doubt, the most successful are those who have self-awareness. Those with self-awareness are often clear on who they are, what their values are, and what priorities they have within their lives. They stand in contrast to those who do not have self-awareness, who may have associated their career with their identity and who often struggle when they transition from that role and are forced to define what's next for them. This shows why self-awareness in particular is so valuable as a basis of all of the other components of GAP.

As I and my team have had the great opportunity of working with people from all careers and all walks of life, one thing remains consistent. Those who develop and increase their self-awareness have a greater ability in developing and increasing all of the other components of GAP, from gravitas to awareness to presence.

That is why *awareness* is the starting point for my research. A wealth of studies and academic theories back up the importance of awareness, and without a thorough understanding of it, progress in GAP enhancement is impossible. Much of this section will provide a basis of academic research around self-awareness, a construct of emotional intelligence, to help you gain the background you need to build your own.

WHERE GAP COMES FROM

The Stanford University Business Advisory Council said that self-awareness was one of the most important competencies leaders should have.[2] The relationship between self-awareness and leadership is relevant to anyone who is or wants to be a leader because studies show that leaders with strong self-awareness have higher performing teams and live a more personally and professionally fulfilled life.[3] Simply, self-awareness is the foundation to mastering your GAP.

Philosophical discussions around the topic of self-awareness have been around for thousands of years. Leaders such as Lao Tzu were recorded saying something along the lines of, "It is wisdom to know others, it is enlightenment to know oneself" as early as the 6th century BCE.[4] But it did not become a studied construct of emotional intelligence until 1972 when Dr. Shelley Duval and Dr. Robert Wicklund published *A Theory of Objective Self-Awareness*. In it, they defined objective self-awareness theory as "when attention is directed inward and the individual's consciousness is focused on himself, he is the object of his own consciousness—hence 'objective' self-awareness."[5] This is where we begin.

UNDERSTANDING SELF-AWARENESS

If a person was randomly asked what they believed *self-awareness* was, they might describe it as the ability to perceive oneself or the ability to understand how others perceive them. Dr. Tasha Eurich, an academic researcher who has spent many years studying self-awareness, defined it as having two parts: internal self-awareness (how well you know yourself) and external self-awareness (how well you understand how others see you).[6] Dr. Roy Baumeister defined self-awareness as "anticipating how others perceive you, evaluating

THE DATA BEHIND GAP

yourself and your actions according to collective beliefs and values, and caring about how others evaluate you."[7] Self-awareness is a category of emotional intelligence that has a direct impact on how you operate in professional situations. Within academic research and studies on self-awareness, we see several terms to describe self-awareness and other similar kinds of emotional intelligence, including the following:

- *Self-Monitoring*: An individual's capacity for monitoring and control of expressive behavior and self-presentation[8]
- *Self-Reflection*: The inspection and evaluation of one's thoughts, feelings, and behavior, which is essential to the process of purposeful and directed cognitional change[9]
- *Managerial Self-Awareness (MSA)*: The ability to reflect on and accurately assess one's own behaviors and skills as they are manifested in workplace interactions[10]
- *Objective Self-Awareness (OSA) Theory*: When attention is directed inward and the individual's consciousness is focused on himself, he is the object of his own consciousness—hence "objective" self-awareness[11]

It is important to understand the different verbiage, phrases, and descriptions researchers use when discussing topics around self-awareness because all of them are relevant to understanding the influences and particulars around mastering your GAP. In later world-class practitioner case studies, you will see some of these, such as self-monitoring and self-reflection, utilized by Robin Rand, Jason Lamb, Dan Cockerell, and others as they share their stories.

SELF-AWARENESS AND PSYCHOLOGY

Self-awareness has been recognized in the fields of psychology, behavioral psychology, and social psychology as a part of emotional intelligence.[12] Studies on this topic have evolved drastically over the last fifty years. In the foundational academic publication on the topic, the 1972 book *A Theory of Objective Self-Awareness*,[13] authors described the objective self-awareness (OSA) theory:

> The orientation of conscious attention was the essence of self-evaluation. Focusing attention on the self brought about objective self-awareness, which initiated an automatic comparison of the self against standards. The *self* was defined very broadly as the person's knowledge of the person.[14]

In 2001, Shelley Duval and Paul Silvia challenged the first findings on the objective OSA theory and proposed new understandings and beliefs, stating, "Self-focused attention is also fundamental to a host of clinical and health phenomena."[15] They further found when people become more self-aware and the feedback they receive has a positive outcome or implication within their lives, they try to be better practitioners of self-awareness. However, if self-awareness provides them with negative feedback, they are more likely to avoid self-awareness to evade the discomfort associated with it. These researchers recognized there were still many uncertainties regarding the topic of self-awareness, specifically how organizational and social psychological standards are internalized by individuals.

I've seen these findings in action in my practice. While I was coaching a mid-level leader within a telecommunications company, we used a peer feedback assessment tool to gain awareness of how others were perceiving her as both a leader and a teammate. For the sake of honesty, coworkers could give feedback anonymously. When she received the results, we connected for a coaching session to methodically go through them to extract as much information as we could. During this process, she became so fixated on some of the critical feedback she received that she became preoccupied with trying to identify who said what about her. Though this was a tool for us to assist her in increasing her self-awareness, she had trouble accepting the critical feedback that was shared with her. The search for self-awareness was resulting in a downturn of self-awareness, a pitfall Duval and Silva had observed in their research. If someone is not consciously comfortable with searching for self-awareness, such as the awareness-enhancement tools we explore later on, this could have negative implications.

Researcher Zuzana Sasovova extended this line of research and sought to uncover the link between self-monitoring, work performance, and social relationships; there were both direct and indirect effects between self-monitoring and an individual's performance. She said,

> Being a high self-monitor is a double-edged sword for ratings of performance. Being a social chameleon allows one to be a friend to many and this may get the high self-monitor an advantage in terms of performance ratings. The cost, however, is that the boundary-spanning social chameleon is more likely to develop outgoing negative ties that are, in turn, detrimental for work performance.[16]

This is yet another potential pitfall for those seeking self-awareness. The primary purpose of this study was to determine the effects of self-monitoring on social relationships as it relates to an individual's performance. Sasovova revealed both positive and negative implications based on the amount of self-awareness an individual has. For GAP practitioners, this underscores that you must have enough self-awareness to identify if you are being a social chameleon. Good, bad, or indifferent, the value is extracted in the knowing of self. This can also assist you in maintaining your authenticity and not jeopardizing your values to be a social chameleon in environments that don't align with who you are.

SELF-AWARENESS AND LEADERSHIP

Self-awareness is a key quality in strong leaders in the workplace. Research has found that effective self-aware leaders have or practice qualities such as humility, integrity, an eagerness to learn, and being team driven. They demonstrate a good understanding of their individual mental states, emotions, sensations, beliefs, desires, and personalities, whereas those who do not have a good understanding of those interpersonal categories are more inclined to be confused and remain directionless as leaders. Researchers Mendemu Showry and K. Manasa stated, "Truly self-aware managers express who they really are and are open to objective feedback that increases their integrity and effectiveness." They quoted researcher A. H. Church, who pointed out that in studies, "high-performing managers were more managerially self-aware compared to average-performing managers."[17] Clearly, there are benefits for leaders demonstrating self-awareness and negative implications for leaders who do not.

While research has shown that many factors contribute to having self-awareness, there is also evidence of obstacles that limit an individual from having self-awareness. Incompetence, negative motives, negative intentions, self-esteem issues, denial, narcissism, egotism, or avoidance are all characteristics that may limit an individual's self-awareness.[18] Self-awareness needs to be an ongoing practice; the individual must consistently evaluate themselves as well as how others perceive or view them. Researcher Scott Taylor contends that external self-awareness is critical because it allows leaders to "accurately read the emotions, thoughts, and preferences of others and the influence they are having on others—how others experience their leader behavior."[19] This is critical for anyone interested in developing gravitas and presence—influencing how others feel around you and your ability to respond to them.

The relationship between self-awareness and leadership has prompted research in several industries with many different outcomes among diverse types of leaders. Most research can be classified under two themes—the effects of a leader's self-awareness on their *individual* leadership performance or on their *organization's* culture and performance. We'll look at a leader's individual performance first.

SELF-AWARENESS AND INDIVIDUAL LEADERSHIP PERFORMANCE

Researcher in managerial psychology Dr. Michael Walton stated, "Much of a person's individual success will be derived from the extent to which they are aware of their own strengths, weaknesses, blind spots and psychological vulnerabilities."[20] In action, this idea has interesting implications. Researchers examined a variety of leaders in the health-care and business industries to analyze individual leadership effectiveness and performance. They concluded that women leaders are no more likely than men to underrate themselves on their level of self-awareness. They also discovered that leaders who underrated themselves actually received higher performance ratings by their direct reports than leaders who overrated themselves, where the effects were the opposite.[21] So while being aware of our flaws may lead us to underrate ourselves initially, that very awareness seems to benefit those we work with.

These results are consistent. In another study, academic students within the United States Naval Academy were measured on their self-awareness and its implications on their leadership behavior and performance. Researchers found that leaders who demonstrated self-awareness had increased performance whereas those who did not had a negative influence on their performance.[22]

Continuing research within academia, workforce MBA students in Los Angeles were analyzed to discover whether "soft-skilled" leadership qualities—such as self-awareness, interpersonal abilities, and communication—were becoming more important and beneficial for private sector leaders. Data collected just a decade ago often indicated that characteristics such as eloquence, charisma, and extroversion (something in between hard and soft skills) were frequently found among corporate business leaders, but research later revealed the benefit of soft-skills leadership qualities, such as self-awareness.[23] And this was not the only educational institution to see the value of soft-skills leadership.

In 2011, Harvard Business School reorganized some of their curriculum to focus more on soft-skills leadership to drive character and competence rather than the traditional hard skills that mainly focused on exclusively academic materials.[24] These two examples indicate that the business world, and more specifically, business schools, are placing a heavier emphasis on soft leadership skills such as self-awareness. Surveys by *Harvard Business Review*, TopMBA.com, and the Association of MBAs have shown that organizations already know they can receive top talent when it comes to hard skills.[25] Therefore, the big differentiator is strong business acumen paired with strong leadership soft skills such as emotional intelligence; our key characteristics gravitas, awareness, presence; and the ability to foster authentic relationships.

Similarly, organizational psychologist Dr. Allan H. Church researched the connection between leaders who demonstrated self-awareness versus leaders who did not and the impact it had on their individual performance at work. To determine this, 134 high-performing and 470 average-performing managers from the technology, pharmaceutical, and airline industries were surveyed using four measurement methods. Church concluded that high performers were significantly more self-aware than average performers.[26] Regardless of the three industries surveyed, leaders who demonstrated effective self-awareness outperformed those who did not.

If a leader is not self-aware, they face other negative implications. When examining managers from different cultures and countries, researchers separated them into individualistic and collectivistic societies. The objective was to identify whether biased self-perceptions would result in leadership derailment, or a leader obstructing others' growth in a work environment. The conclusion? Those with tendencies to be self-enhancing or self-diminishing varied greatly, and depending on what tendency the leader had, it could result in a positive, negative, or neutral outcome on leadership performance.[27] This provides a heightened sense of relevance to leaders who operate at a global level or have functions that require working with multiple cultures. An increase in your awareness can assist you in identifying cultural considerations to account for in your business dynamics and functions.

Misconceptions or a lack of a leader's self-awareness can also lead to leadership illusions. Author and professor D. D. Warrick defined a negative implication of leadership illusions—when the leader is "seeing something different than it is."[28] When someone has such an illusion about their self-awareness, they tend to make decisions that are less likely to succeed and that affect their ability to grow as a leader within their organization.

An article by professor and human resources researcher Cam Caldwell focused on the connection between false depictions and leadership effects, specifically how self-deception can create barriers to self-awareness and conflict with one's identity. These barriers can keep a leader from performing at their highest level. Self-deception, the "denial of the duty owed to the self when it causes an individual to avoid confronting the need to modify one's behavior,"[29] is often viewed as a leader's compromising action that obstructs their ability to become more self-aware and receive feedback from teammates that could help the leader implement changes to assist in their personal development. When a leader lacks self-awareness, their organization can institute feedback mechanisms and reviews, but the feedback may not be received well, analyzed, or applied.[30]

This is a problem that often spurs companies to seek leadership training, development, and coaching for their team members. Leadership coaching has been emerging as a form of continuous development for leaders around the globe and throughout all sectors and industries. That's one of the many reasons I am passionate about my career: We get to see the same principles in action across all environments. The International Coaching Federation defined leadership coaching as "partnering with clients in a leadership position in a thought-provoking and creative process that inspires them to maximize their personal and professional potential."[31] Researchers found that when a leader engages in leadership coaching, it assists in their development of self-awareness, which has led to higher individual performance.[32]

Leadership coaching requires a masterful practitioner, often one with decades of experience in leadership positions themselves and certified in coaching to assist another leader to unlock their maximum potential and embrace the possible. Since launching my leadership training and coaching firm, Victory Strategies, I have seen executive and leadership coaching become more normalized in organizations. Interestingly, but not surprisingly, I have also witnessed many organizations begin to offer executive and leadership coaching alignments within their positional compensation packages; the training is a perk that comes with a new job, aimed at employee retention, faster organizational alignment, and increased performance. This reflects a recent study by McKinsey, which identified one of the top reasons an employee will leave their company is because of a lack of organizational investment in their education and growth.[33] I'll never forget a longtime B2B client of ours sharing that one of their senior executives received a competitive offer from a competing firm, but he turned the offer down because he valued the coaching our firm provides so much, and he appreciated his organization's investment in him. With the job market becoming increasingly competitive, leadership and executive coaching continues to prove to be a competitive advantage.

When I explain the role of a coach to new clients, one of the resources I use is the following modified chart from *Harvard Business Review* to explain some of the coaching differences and dynamics as it compares to consulting and therapy.[34] Though coaching sometimes can be perceived as consulting or therapy, it isn't. Coaching is a partnership (defined as an alliance, not a legal business partnership) between the coach and the client in a thought-provoking and creative process that inspires the client to maximize personal and professional potential. It is designed to facilitate the creation and development of goals and to develop and carry out a plan for achieving those goals. This is exactly the frame of mind from which we will approach GAP in this book.

Consulting		Coaching		Therapy
Paid to come up with the answers	Advises individual leaders on business matters	Focuses on the future	Paid to ask right questions	Focuses on the past
Focuses on organizational performance	Involves management in goal setting	Fosters individual performance in a business context	Tackles difficult issues at work and home	Diagnoses and treats dysfunctionality
Strives for objectivity	Based on organizational ethics	Helps executives discover their own path	Focuses on individual behavioral change	Based on medical ethics
Provides quantitative analysis of problems	Paid for by the company		Explores subjective experience	Paid for by the individual

Executive and leadership coaching goes beyond the positive impacts of an individual leader's self-awareness and performance. These kinds of coaching include focus on self-awareness, which can also affect teammates within their organization.[35] But how?

SELF-AWARENESS AND ORGANIZATIONAL CULTURE AND PERFORMANCE

Many studies connecting self-awareness to leadership observed the effects that self-awareness has on an organization's culture and performance. One group of studies explored the idea of authentic leadership. What characteristics are required of a leader to achieve it? A common theme emerged: self-awareness. *Authentic leadership* includes self-awareness, unbiased processing (the ability to process information in a neutral and emotionally regulated way), authentic behavior and actions, and relational authenticity. The researchers specifically looked at the effects self-aware leaders had on their followers within their organization. They found "authentic leaders influence followers' well-being through emotions: authentic leaders provide an atmosphere conducive to the experience of positive emotions, and their own positive emotions influence followers' experiences."[36] In other words, if a leader is leading a team in an authentic way where they can connect with their team members, it will increase the performance of the team through motivated behaviors.

Within the health-care industry, self-awareness among physicians and health-care leaders has produced many organizational benefits. For instance, research has found that physician leaders with self-awareness can positively impact their organizations, resulting in improved patient safety, reverse patient mortality, and better development among junior trainees.[37] Research at a hospital in the Netherlands showed that individual leaders with self-awareness and the ability to understand how others perceived them created stronger relationships with their peers, increasing organizational performance through patient safety, hospital functionality, and the patient experience. Again, we see self-awareness building gravitas and presence in the workplace.

The relationship of self-awareness and leadership affects the business sector as well. It was observed that "leaders' self-awareness of their own leadership style influenced their employee's satisfaction, self-leadership, and leader effectiveness."[38] Researchers followed 48 leaders in unspecified positions and 222 of their direct reports, trying to pinpoint the effects of a leader who demonstrates strong self-awareness when it came to empowering leadership—a leader's ability to empower their team members to understand their roles, responsibilities, and authorities to execute their job requirements. Consistent with previous research, the study found that leaders who demonstrated self-awareness or underrated their leadership were identified as more effective leaders by their followers than those who answered oppositely. The most important implication was that a leader's self-awareness affects their own behavioral outcomes and satisfaction with their direct reports and team. I would later find these results confirmed in my own research.

Leadership awareness also plays a key role in times of change within an organization. When two researchers sought to identify why failure occurs within organizations when change is being implemented, they interviewed leaders from thirty-three different organizations in the UK, from industries including business, the public sector, global organizations, and small community businesses. The researchers wanted to measure a leader's effectiveness with change implementation. They discovered that "blindness" to organizational systems or a focus on their own ego led some leaders into "traps" that seriously damaged the success of change interventions. They were lacking *situational* awareness—one of the four components of awareness. Leaders who were involved in successful change efforts and avoided these traps displayed behaviors that demonstrated high levels of self- and situational awareness, an ability to "work in the moment," and the capacity to remain in tune with the overall purpose of the change. Again, we see awareness leading directly to the kind of *presence* a leader needs. The authors of the study also found that these leaders were better at recognizing how to effectively use their specific abilities within the organizational change.[39] Leaders lacking self-awareness were not as successful in leading the organization—or even small groups— through a successful change implementation. They also could be obstructed from positive foresight when responsible for leading organizational or departmental change, which could make them feel detached from their organization and its team members.[40] The takeaway here is that self-aware leaders often have a higher probability of success in implementing change or innovation for themselves or for leading change management as a leader of others.

AWARE, DON'T CARE

After thoroughly exploring all the research available on self-awareness, I found I wanted to dive deeper for answers to several questions that didn't exist in the research pertaining to leadership self-awareness. Specifically, I wondered:

- What are the implications for a leader who is self-aware but just doesn't care how they are perceived by others?
- Does self-awareness differ between leaders based on a leader's tenure in a leadership role or how experienced they are?
- Does the self-awareness of a leader influence trust and communication alignment within their team?
- Regardless of the leader's self-awareness levels, does the perception of the leader's colleagues matter?
- Does working for a leader lacking self-awareness increase the turnover intention of the leader's team members?

To discover the answers, I started a five-year process of research that examined leaders in industries such as consulting, finance, furniture, health care, law enforcement, real estate, and technology. Each leader was physically located within the United States but operated teams, people, and business units throughout the world. To conduct this research, I created an academically tested survey assessment to be completed by both the leader and one or more of their teammates to measure the leader's self-awareness (and whether the leader overrated or underrated themselves) along with the implications those scores indicated. An *overrater* meant the leader rated themselves higher than their direct reports or teammates rated them on the self-awareness scale; an *underrater* meant the leader rated themselves lower than their direct reports or teammates did.

The results mirrored previous research on the subject. Leaders who were overraters earned lower trust and higher turnover intention of those they led; underraters earned greater trust and lower turnover intention. Interestingly, overraters were perceived to be better communicators. One explanation for this may be that overraters seemed to exude confidence and were more vocal with their team members than underraters. On the other hand, overraters may be perceived as arrogant, having blind spots or lacking authentic confidence by their teammates and direct reports. Underraters, with their implied humility, might not thoroughly understand how their direct reports saw them as less vocal. From my research, I gathered that being an underrater is "second best" to being a leader with self-awareness because it could be perceived as an area of humility. It is important to note that regardless of being an underrater or overrater, if still lacking self-awareness, leaders with underrater results are preferred for individual and team performance.

Each leader used a self-monitoring assessment survey so I could understand if their self-awareness scores were authentically accurate. Self-monitoring assessments are assessments that measure if an individual has the ability to monitor their own behavior and how it is being perceived or to contort it to drive a specific outcome. They're a great way to identify whether a leader is perfectly aware of themselves but just simply does not care how others perceive them. I call this, "aware, don't care." The data from the self-awareness assessments seems to tell us that effective self-monitoring indicates a positive relationship with one's self-awareness.

In support of existing literature and research, we found that a leader's self-awareness influences the trust of their team, specifically their direct reports. Regardless of a leader's actual self-awareness, if their direct reports *perceive* they are lacking self-awareness, it negatively affects the leader's verbal workplace communication and trust, increasing the turnover intention of their direct reports. Empirical evidence in existing literature has shown that a leader's self-awareness—or lack thereof—can affect the performance of themselves and their teams, positively or negatively.[41] A self-aware leader is more beneficial to performance than one who is not.

My next question was whether leadership experience was related to a leader's self-awareness levels (whether more experienced leaders had more self-awareness). To measure this, and the potential implications it could have on team member trust and verbal workplace communication, participants were divided into three categories of leadership length: nine years or less, ten to twenty years, and twenty or more years. Overall, these categories were close to an even distribution, and the average age of the leaders was forty-seven. The data found that leaders with experience of between ten and twenty years had the highest level of self-awareness. They also had the highest levels of team member trust (75 percent), effective verbal workplace communication (85 percent), and team members with little intention to leave (85 percent). Of course, every leader is different regardless of years of experience in a leadership role. But when categorically analyzed, leaders who had led between ten and twenty years had better scores across the board than leaders with under nine years or twenty plus years of leadership experience. This means leaders in the under-nine and over-twenty years of leadership tenure categories should be on high alert, as statistically they are more likely to lack self-awareness than their leader counterparts with ten to twenty years of leadership experience. We will dive deeper into this throughout part 3, when we explore tools for mastering your own GAP.

As you start to master your GAP, strengthening gravitas, awareness, and presence in your own life, it's important to have an understanding of how self-awareness is key to your success. The information in this chapter is aimed at helping you understand the how and why—the academic and scientific research that shows the implications self-awareness can have on a leader's GAP. Leadership development, training, and coaching, as well as other mechanisms, are important to increase self-monitoring capacity, self-awareness levels, and self-control abilities. By analyzing research findings, you are better equipped with the knowledge of just how vital the perception of their self-awareness and competence is to their direct reports and those they work alongside. With this knowledge, you can identify areas of focus when it comes to you and your team's development trainings.

People's perception is their reality. If teammates perceive leaders as lacking self-awareness, it mitigates their ability to trust and communicate with their leaders and negatively affects the team's performance, regardless of how high a leader rates in self-awareness. Teammates' perception of their leader's self-awareness also can influence their desire to stay with the organization; if team members decide to leave because of how they perceive their leaders, it could decrease the organization's retention rates, ultimately wasting a substantial amount of time and resources. Therefore, leaders need to not only strive for self-awareness and self-monitoring abilities but also be conscious of how they are perceived by their peers, direct reports, and teammates. The GAP of a leader has direct implications for the leader's individual and team performance.

Many leaders believe they have leadership self-awareness, but statistically, they do not.[42] You can probably recall leaders you've had who you perceived to be lacking self-awareness. There is good news though: A leader can grow in self-awareness with a conscious and intentional commitment.

Everybody is a leader. A leader of self, family, community, and sometimes in a professional capacity and of others. Regardless of whether you are early or late in your career or if you consider yourself a leader or not, increased self-awareness is scientifically proven to enhance your abilities to be successful in your endeavors. The research included in this book can also enhance your emotional intelligence, improve your leadership self-awareness, and, of course, lead you to mastering your GAP. Now join me in seeing how these experts have experienced GAP in their careers.

PART 2

WORLD-CLASS PRACTITIONER GAP CASE STUDIES

*W*hen you picture a great leader, who or what do you see? For many, it's someone like Alexander the Great—one of history's most well-known leaders. And if you look back at his origins, you see many of the elements of GAP in action in a pretty spectacular way. Just out of his teens, Alexander assumed the throne of Macedonia from his father, and by the age of thirty he had created one of the largest empires in the history of the world, stretching from Greece to northwestern India. Undefeated in battle, historians have called him one of the greatest military leaders to have ever walked the face of the earth…and he accomplished all this in his twenties. Alexander the Great was a continuous practitioner of the practice I now call the GAP Enhancement Cycle: educate, experiment, and evaluate. From an early age, Alexander was taught by his father and exposed to environments, people, situations, and battles, allowing him to absorb as much information and detail as possible before evaluating the situations and scenarios in private later. Just like you, Alexander's father understood the importance of studying and becoming aware of the complexities of leadership qualities—our gravitas, awareness, and presence—before attempting to implement these learnings with his son.

As a newly crowned leader at twenty, Alexander continued to allocate and prioritize time each day to study history and philosophy with his teachers. He understood the value of reflection, creative thought, and learning from others. Through the lens of *awareness*, Alexander knew that many of his military generals associated philosophy with weakness. Therefore, anytime Alexander engaged in philosophical lessons, he ensured his generals were unaware of it to control their perception of his *gravitas*. The thoughtfulness and intentionality Alexander the Great consistently practiced enabled him to be one of the greatest leaders in history… and much of his success can be attributed to his *gravitas, awareness,* and *presence.*

And now, we see these timeless traits fueling the success of the modern-day leaders you are about to meet.

As someone who is consistently in the incubator of educating, experimenting, and evaluating my own gravitas, awareness, and presence, I believe GAP is not just an acronym but also has a symbolic and literal meaning: I often see a real gap between a practitioner's ability to rise from good to great. We are here to overcome that gap. Having coached thousands of leaders and worked with hundreds of organizations, I often engage with professionals who have either self-identified or seen in feedback that they are lacking a component of the secret formula we refer to as gravitas, awareness, and presence. Within professional environments, I've found the components of GAP often come up in conversation, feedback sessions, performance improvement plans, or as components necessary for success. Yet, despite so many people using these words in their vocabulary, they often have difficulty articulating exactly *what it is, how to develop it,* and *how to put it into practice.*

In this section, you will learn from close to thirty world-class practitioners—men and women who have mastered their GAP. You will see how the theory and research included in chapter 1 is put into practice before you develop a playbook of your own in part 3. Here in part 2, each practitioner shares a specific story or experience from their career that delivers lessons and takeaways on the facets of gravitas, awareness, and presence. Each case study is a lived experience; many share similar themes, takeaways, epiphanies, and lessons learned, emphasizing the importance of repeated takeaways gathered through experience. If you read each case through the lens of curiosity, I am confident you will gain wisdom-filled takeaways that you can apply as a practitioner yourself to enhance your GAP capabilities.

CHAPTER 2

GRAVITAS

The influence, emotions, and feelings someone's demeanor evokes in others.

CREDIBILITY CAN BE A LIABILITY
Scott Campbell, USAF Colonel and TOPGUN Fighter Pilot Instructor

Scott (who goes by the call sign "Soup") had just become the wing commander of Davis-Monthan United States Air Force (USAF) Base in Tucson, Arizona. A wing commander is essentially the CEO of the base and all the human capital, equipment, and resources associated with the base. Approximately .05 percent of USAF officers become wing commanders, making it a prestigious and highly respected position. It just so happened that the Davis-Monthan USAF Base is one of the air force's prized jewels. It is the largest A-10 aircraft base, and almost every pilot who has ever flown the A-10 in the US Air Force has been stationed at or trained on this base at some point. Taking command meant that for the next two years, Scott would oversee the billions of dollars in resources at this base, lead up to eleven thousand personnel, and report directly to his three-star general superior.

Up until then, Scott had established quite a reputation, not only in the US Air Force but also in the fighter pilot community. As a young officer, Scott was selected to attend the prestigious US Air Force Weapons School, equivalent to the US Navy Fighter Weapons School, referred to as TOPGUN. The USAF Weapons School produced the best pilots in the military, and approximately a year after Scott graduated, he deployed in a significant combat operation in March of 2002 that earned him three Distinguished Flying Cross awards, the USAF's highest achievement next to the Medal of Honor. Scott later returned to the USAF Weapons School, became an instructor, and accumulated more than three thousand flight hours over the next decade.

In Scott's first days of command, he made it a point to share some of his expectations with his staff. To remain qualified as a pilot, Scott needed to stay current with the USAF's flight hour training and requirements. Because of the rigor demanded from wing commanders, it was not uncommon for leaders to complete just the bare minimum in training requirements. Scott pointed out that when the pilots conducted training flights in formation, the easiest place to be with the least amount of training or technical abilities was on one of the farthest sides of the airplane formation. So, it was not abnormal for previous wing commanders to join these training formations and assume such a position. As you can imagine, a lot of preparation goes into making an aircraft ready to fly, and after flight, it is routine for the pilots to immediately debrief and identify areas for improvement. Through Scott's years of service, he witnessed many wing commanders who took the farthest side in an aircraft formation often skip the debrief by reason of their demanding schedule. Keeping this in mind, Scott said to himself, "If I ever become a wing commander, I am going to make it a point to *lead* flight formations when I fly and show my team that I will continue to operate within the normal pilot protocols and expectations."

Therefore, one of his team's expectations was simple; when Scott was going to fly in formation with the other pilots, he would not be on the farthest side of the formation. Instead, he would be leading it as the instructor in a technical position that required more intimate planning, processes, and responsibilities. Scott's staff heard him loud and clear. For his first six months in command, the base's culture began to appreciate that Scott had a different leadership style and approach. His staff caught a sense of gravitas and integrity in the way he led.

As this started to become routine, Scott, the highest-ranking leader, received an order from the USAF leadership that he and his team were to conduct a massive rehearsal exercise for a possible real-world operation. This exercise included close to three thousand personnel and 135 aircraft. After weeks of planning, the training rehearsal was ready to execute, and Scott's team listed him on the flight manifest as the lead aircraft of the main flight formation. Concentrating on so many other tasks and items, Scott did not give the assignment much thought until the days leading up to it. The requirements and technical abilities required for the responsibility of lead aircraft were high, and though Scott had the experience, flight hours, and credibility, he was not flying every single day due to the demands of leadership. He was not performing hundreds of repetitions as were many other pilots who had the newest technology. Nonetheless, when go-time came, Scott got into the cockpit of his aircraft and led the formation.

As the training operation progressed, Scott led his formation through a planned high-risk challenge that required the pilots fly at 400 miles per hour only 100 feet off the ground. He had a thought at that exact moment: *I am not the person who should be leading this formation. Compared to the other pilots, I have the lowest proficiency right now. This is stupid.*

Thankfully, Scott and his teammates concluded the training operation successfully, but when he joined his team for the debrief, he pulled aside his most trusted staff members and said,

"I still plan on flying as a flight lead and instructor pilot in the formations when I fly, but we—and I—cannot let my credibility become a liability. My experience does not equal my current proficiency."

Scott's Takeaways

1. You Need to Be Aware of Your Gravitas

Taking command of Davis-Monthan Air Force Base, Scott was a living legend to some. He had been in combat, instructed the world's best pilots, and earned three Distinguished Flying Cross awards (and to receive one is legendary). Reflecting on this, Scott emphasized how important it was for leaders to objectively look at how others might view them based on their accomplishments. Equally as important is for the leader to identify how knowing how others view them might affect their own ego and self-confidence. He continued to act like a leader in formation, when by his own admission later, his team would have been better served by him taking a position farther out. By being aware of the influence your gravitas can have on those you interact with, you can make more composed decisions that are objectively the best for the team.

2. Credibility Can Become a Liability

With such "textbook" fighter pilot accomplishments, Scott had credibility within the USAF as someone who had almost done it all. And while it can often be a morale booster for those following a leader with such credibility, Scott pointed out that it can also be a liability. If people—particularly those who follow you—believe you have seen it all, done it all, and know it all, it can create an environment of complacency in how they may challenge you, question you, or think critically with you. Neither Scott nor his staff thought anything of it when they placed him in the lead formation position because that was his expectation when he first took command. As Scott quickly realized while in the throes of the training operation, there were better pilots on his team who were more proficient in the technical requirements to lead the formation than he was.

3. Experience Is Not the Same as Proficiency

Scott had to be the most proficient fighter pilot to become credible, and once that was established and tested, he advanced in rank and leadership responsibilities. An increase in rank and leadership responsibilities as a USAF officer, particularly a pilot, meant he would have less time in the aircraft, which ultimately means less up-to-date proficiency. Scott's example reminds us that many leaders learn technical skills and responsibilities to be successful at a specific part of their job. As their success continues, they often advance to leadership levels that demand less technical tasks and more leadership responsibilities and requirements. As time goes on, the trainings, changes, and innovations of the technical job continue to progress, but because a leader is no longer consistently doing the technical job every day, their up-to-date proficiency diminishes.

Gravitas Takeaway

Be cautious of your own gravitas—both in how it affects you and others.

READY OR NOT, YOU'RE CEO
Jerry Morgan, CEO and Board Member of Texas Roadhouse Inc.

On March 18, 2021, Jerry Morgan was notified that Kent Taylor, Texas Roadhouse's founder and CEO, had unexpectedly passed away. As the new president of the company, Jerry was still getting used to the demands of leadership. Within hours, Jerry boarded a plane and flew to Texas Roadhouse's headquarters in Louisville, Kentucky. Upon arrival, Jerry learned that Kent had written a note specifying that Jerry be named CEO. In the hours that followed, the board voted to support Kent's endorsement, and Jerry was named CEO of Texas Roadhouse and its nearly seven hundred restaurant locations.

Jerry, an athlete in high school, was a longtime veteran of the food service industry. He valued the team camaraderie required to get food to the customers in a timely manner without jeopardizing quality. He had entered the food service industry starting at Burger King, working alongside his admired and respected uncle who had recently purchased a handful of Burger Kings in Texas. In 1986, Jerry was managing twenty-five team members in his Burger King location, which was producing $1.7 million in annual revenue. His career was progressing in the right direction, and Jerry felt his future was with his uncle and Burger King—until his uncle unexpectedly passed away in an airplane accident. Jerry left Burger King and joined Bennigan's. After much success, Jerry joined Texas Roadhouse in 1997 as a managing partner and opened its first location in Texas. Four years later, he earned Texas Roadhouse's highest award, Managing Partner of the Year, and his career within the company accelerated. In 2014, Jerry was promoted to regional market partner, leading 120 restaurants in fourteen states within the United States. In December 2020, Jerry was named president of Texas Roadhouse.

When Jerry became president, informal discussions with Kent led to a decision: This would be the beginning of a three- to five-year plan for Jerry to learn everything he needed to before becoming CEO. After Kent's unfortunate passing, Jerry's timeline had shrunk from five years to one, and without any intentional preparation, Jerry became CEO almost overnight. Taking on the CEO role of an iconic brand like Texas Roadhouse was no small task, especially when the company was still hurting from Kent's passing. Kent created Texas Roadhouse's entire identity. Their slogan is, "Legendary food, legendary service," and their team members are affectionately known as "roadies." Jerry had to ask himself, *How do I heal a hurting company to continue Kent's legendary reputation and vision for this organization and its roadies?* Jerry was determined to continue Kent's mission and legacy with his first task: company healing.

One of the first things Jerry did when he became CEO was write a letter to the entire organization, or as he called them, "Roadie Nation." Jerry wanted all his team members to know he was hurting with them and that he needed their help to be successful in executing Kent's vision for continued growth and success. The response was overwhelmingly positive, and this single act ignited a spark of motivation to propel Texas Roadhouse into the future. He had begun with honesty, and it radiated through his gravitas, which the entire organization could feel.

I asked Jerry whether he realized any significant or noticeable change after becoming CEO. "Yes—everyone within the company became overly nice to me." This realization made Jerry more self-aware regarding how others perceived him because of his title and the gravitas that came with it. This self-awareness led to an increase in Jerry's situational awareness every time he entered a room of roadies. He had to become more intentional with how he was showing up if he wanted authentic interactions with his team members.

Jerry's Takeaway

1. **Know Yourself So When Opportunity Presents Itself, You're Ready**

   Jerry has always tried to be aware of his driving values and what he prioritizes as a leader. Treating team members—regardless of position within the organization—as valuable partners and with respect has helped motivate team members to work hard and remain committed to the mission of the organization. A question Jerry regularly asks himself is, *What do I want to be known for when I leave the company?* This simple question allows him to realign his values, intention, and actions to ensure he is showing up every day to see that mission through. Jerry doesn't just want success for himself and his team; he wants them all to be *highly* successful, so frequently checking in with himself

to maintain an appropriate degree of self-awareness is a key
to his sustained success.

2. **Starting from the Bottom Has Value**

   In our fast-paced, driven, and competitive economy, people
   often ask themselves how to get to the top as soon as possible.
   But Jerry is a living example of the value that can come from
   growing through nearly every function of a business before
   becoming a leader. During our time together, Jerry shared
   with me that he often sees CEOs or senior executives in the
   food service industry become almost uncomfortable when
   they leave the corporate headquarters and walk into one of
   their restaurant locations, but Jerry isn't. Because Jerry was
   once a kitchen manager himself, he feels very comfortable
   when he walks into one of Texas Roadhouse's nearly seven
   hundred locations. He's been there, knows the environment,
   knows the functions, knows the realities of the customer
   interactions, and therefore feels very confident in meeting
   every roadie where they are in discussion, in mindset, and
   in function. "Nothing energizes me more than spending
   time at our restaurants," Jerry said.

3. **Doubt and Humility Are Your Friends**

   "Any leader who says they don't ever doubt themselves is full
   of crap," said Jerry. That doubt is a healthy self-awareness
   and allows a leader to be intentional about their capabilities,
   strengths, and weaknesses. When Jerry became CEO, he
   quickly realized that almost all his experience in the industry
   was as an operator, not as a corporate leader, so he had a
   lot to learn—and fast. He sought counsel from some trusted
   board members, advisers, and colleagues to assist him in
   building his corporate acumen so he could best serve his
   teammates and their clients. When reflecting on his experience so far, Jerry left me with his greatest motivation of
   all: "I just don't want to let Kent or Roadie Nation down."

Gravitas Takeaway

Every single experience and repetition you engage with throughout your life will better prepare you for what's next. Treasure and embrace the gift of experience. It has the ability to put your gravitas in strong standing before ever taking on an elevated role.

BRIEFING THE ADMIRAL
Jason Lamb, US Air Force Intelligence Officer of the Year

*J*ason had prepared for a year and a half to give an informational and intelligence presentation to Admiral Dennis Blair, the four-star United States Navy admiral in charge of the Pacific theater of operation. In 1999, it was the largest theater in the US military. Jason, a young officer in the air force, was told that the presentation was the most important one of his career up to that point.

Jason had graduated from the US Air Force Academy and began a promising career in intelligence. In 1999, the US military identified that gaining competence and understanding of one particular country was a high priority for the sake of global stability and security. Jason was tasked with gathering as much intelligence as he could about the air capabilities of that country to brief to the admiral. He had eighteen months to compile research, visit national intelligence agencies and think tanks, and prepare a first-of-its-kind exhaustive comparative analysis. Jason had never created anything like it, let alone presented it to an officer of such rank and stature.

Throughout the next eighteen months, Jason heard bits and pieces about the admiral and welcomed any information he could gather to prepare him for expectations the admiral might have of the presentation and its contents. All the feedback was the same: The admiral was brilliant, well-connected—including having a personal relationship with the president of the United States—and was unswervingly focused on the topic Jason was to present.

When the day finally came to present to Admiral Blair and his staff, Jason felt confident in his materials but a bit uncertain about his ability to present them well. Jason arrived in the briefing room early and began setting up his presentation. The staff and team members in the room were conversing while Jason faced his presentation screen to ensure the slide transitions were working correctly. Suddenly, Jason could *feel* the room change, like it suddenly had a new center of gravity. The admiral had entered.

"Room, attention!" was called out and the admiral swiftly said, "At ease. Please take your seats." The admiral sat at the head of the table and then turned to look at Jason, quickly appraising his youth and his junior rank.

Anticipating Jason's feelings, the admiral smiled at him, made a few remarks that emphasized he was human, and then allowed Jason to begin. The admiral had made Jason feel comfortable enough to present on his expertise rather than intimidate him. Throughout the presentation, Admiral Blair asked thoughtful and specific questions that showed he was present, thoroughly prepared, and completely engaged in the information Jason was transmitting. The nearly two-hour presentation felt like ten minutes to Jason. When it concluded, the admiral smiled and said to Jason,

"Thank you, that's good work," and then exited the room. It was a success. Jason felt exhausted and elated, and he was committed to continuing in the US Air Force.

US Navy Admiral Dennis Blair

In the four years Jason was in the US Air Force before this experience, he had been led by a handful of people who made him feel undervalued and unappreciated. They seemed focused on their careers and tended to neglect their people. Jason had always wanted to be an officer, but was uncertain if he was going to continue. Engaging with a leader in the military with the highest rank showed him what was possible. Unlike the others, this leader was fully engaged with him, making him feel both challenged and valued. The experience reignited his passion and motivation to lead others and make the military a career instead of a short duty of service. Jason shared, "If it wasn't for my exposure to that kind of admirable leadership, I don't know if I would have stayed in the military for over twenty-five years." Jason's highly accomplished career includes earning four master's degrees, leading teams of more than 650 personnel throughout four continents, and being recognized as the US Air Force Intelligence Officer of the Year 2000. As a senior leader, at the rank of colonel, Jason became famous for his work in fundamentally challenging and shifting the culture of the six-hundred-thousand-member US Air Force, culminating in leveraging his insights to advise the air force chief of staff on how to best mitigate significant disconnects between values and mission alignment to create a better culture for the entire air force. Who knows if any of the above would have been possible if Jason hadn't been engaged by a leader who inspired him to continue his career. But that might just be the power of a leader's gravitas and its influence on emerging and developing leaders.

Jason's Takeaways

1. Gravitas Is like Gravity

Jason will never forget how everyone felt the admiral's physical presence when he entered the room. Was it due to people's biases and beliefs about the admiral? Was it starstruck theories of how a four-star engages with others? Jason had engaged with senior officers but never a four-star officer—who had the same reputation as a *Fortune* 500 CEO, except with rank, power, and military might. When Jason reflected on what everyone felt when the admiral entered the room, he shared, "The admiral exuded confidence but not arrogance, personal authority, genuine expression in his mannerisms, gestures, and facial expressions—all of which contributed to us relaxing because we could relate to his humanity. He wasn't superhuman. He was just more experienced, and he was aware of that, which allowed him to put everyone in the room at ease knowing he was there to seek understanding, listen, and collaborate—not dictate."

2. **Be Intentional About Your Communication—Verbal and Nonverbal**

When you enter a room or environment as a senior leader in any organization, people are "standing by" to see how they should respond to, engage with, and act around you. If you are leading the people in the room, chances are, it really matters to them how they come across to you. Often, this can lead to a lot of advance preparation of materials as well as cleaning and polishing the environment. By being self- and situationally aware of the environment and the possibilities of how your team members *feel*, you can be more intentional with your verbal and nonverbal communication. Are you positively or negatively influencing their potential anxiety, nervousness, and mindset? What are you doing when you enter an environment to make your people feel how you want them to feel?

3. **Reset Between Environments**

As Jason grew in rank and tenure in the military, he realized how frequently leaders are exposed to negative updates in one meeting before advancing to the next scheduled meeting. Reflecting on that and his experience with the admiral many years prior, he shared, "It is so important for a leader to consistently reset their emotional composure in between meetings so that any emotions evoked in their previous meeting are not carried into their next meeting. One thing I do is take five minutes between each meeting to mentally reset, become present in how I am feeling, and then try to center myself to go into my next meeting composed, in control, and as close to neutral with my emotions as I can be. Practitioner tip: I would often splash water on my face in the bathroom between meetings to associate the mental reset with a physical reset. Plus, it made my physical appearance look fresher."

Gravitas Takeaway

Micro details, actions, and components of gravitas can enhance or diminish an environment and those around you. Thoughtfulness can play a strong role in which outcome prevails.

"50 PERCENT OF MY TIME IN THE BOARDROOM WAS GAP"
Diana Markaki-Bartholdi, Founder and CEO of The Boardroom

*A*t thirty-seven years old, Diana exited her first board meeting with a Greek-based, multinational, publicly traded construction company feeling other-than-normal; the new environment had unknown expectations, and she was the youngest in the room. With years of experience as a global attorney, Diana recognized she had never felt this way before and was motivated to identify the root cause.

After completing her law degree in her home country of Greece, Diana trained as an international lawyer in New York City at a large, globally recognized law firm. Over the next fifteen years, Diana gained experience operating as an international lawyer in the United States, United Kingdom, Italy, Greece, and Switzerland.

Being well versed in many different dynamics of global commerce and fluent in several languages, Diana established her credibility as someone who could adapt to many environments, read the room she was in, and approach any obstacle through a global lens. So, when she was approached to join her first board of directors outside of a firm she had been operating in as a stakeholder, she grew excited at the growth opportunity. During Diana's first meeting, she quickly identified that she was the youngest and was one of only two women on the ten-person board. Wanting to conform, Diana started attending boardroom meetings wearing dark earth-colored clothing, because that was how many of the other (predominantly male) board members were dressed. When Diana spoke at these meetings, she tried to make her voice sound deeper to assert confidence and maturity and to create the perception that she was perhaps older than she was. The dynamic was not any less stressful with a proxy battle that the organization became involved in during Diana's first board meeting. After a few months, Diana didn't recognize herself in those board meetings. By trying to be someone she was not, she—and the board members—realized that she was departing from her credibility and the reasons she had been asked to join outside the boardroom.

Through thoughtful and intentional reflection, Diana began to find her natural identity. She recognized she was not assisting any women who would join the board after her because she was not creating realistic expectations of how and why women leaders are valuable to boardrooms. "People know when you are not being authentic, and that creates a hesitant environment, especially in boardrooms," Diana said. Every person on the board had something unique to offer the organization and was credible in their own way based on their experiences. To make that work, she needed to leave her ego at the door and be authentically herself, bringing her real gravitas, awareness, and presence to the room.

Doing just that, Diana found success on the board, leading to an additional board opportunity with an investment fund. This time, Diana was the only woman on the board. With up-to-date situational awareness, Diana saw that there was a large imbalance in board representation worldwide; a large majority of board members were mostly white men. To create a community of male *and* female leaders with the credibility and experience to sit on boards, Diana founded The Boardroom—a pan-European club for women executives who aspired to be board members. Diana's organization also includes male members who champion this initiative and provide valuable perspective with board experience. At the time of this writing, The Boardroom operates in five countries throughout Europe and continues to assist executives in developing their boardroom GAP.

During our interview, Diana transparently shared with me that 50 percent of the time she is in a boardroom (if not more) she is engaging each component of GAP because the environment and stakes of the decisions in the environment depend on it.

Diana's Takeaways

1. **Courageous Presence: Balancing Authenticity and Conformity**

   Specific environments demand certain roles and expectations. Attire, for instance, is often expected to be somewhat uniform depending on location, function, and industry. Professionals working on Wall Street or in a law firm often wear business attire, whereas professionals in Silicon Valley often wear casual attire. Specific topics of conversation might also be inappropriate. Often, topics like sex, drugs, religion, or politics may not be suitable in a professional work environment. Whether the topics discussed or the attire worn, it is important to identify the professional expectations of the environment you are working within. Through the four components of awareness, gaining a competent baseline of these expectations allows you to prepare accordingly and can enhance the perception others have of your professionalism and gravitas.

Diana points out that awareness will assist you in identifying what level of conformity is appropriate and also what level of authenticity is appropriate through the presence you bring to your environment. Authenticity is most often valuable when it comes to your personality, beliefs, morals, ethics, and integrity. Authenticity can be a superpower in differentiating yourself (especially on a board) from others. But, when taken to extremes, the kind of "authenticity" that comes in, for example, showering only once a week or not conforming in any capacity to the expectations of your work environment because that's "who you authentically are" is most likely a misinterpretation of authenticity. Authentic presence is built on awareness of yourself, the environment you are operating within, and the way you interact with others.

Throughout our interview discussion, Diana expressed that continuous effort is required to find balance in understanding the right intersection between authenticity and conformity so you can play by the rules while also leveraging the unique experiences, values, and beliefs that got you to the table in the first place.

2. **Recognizing the Need for Change (Social Awareness)**

Inventors create a product that fulfills a need in the market. Innovators transform a product or industry to compete in the future. High-performing board members recognize what is required for tomorrow's success. With the social awareness necessary to determine the expectations of government, consumers, and regulators, a board can be more thoughtful in their foresight and decisions. Diana pointed out how understanding the priorities of society and its consumers as well as upskilling in artificial intelligence and technology are a few examples of how social awareness will enable tomorrow's successes.

3. **Knowing Self Assists with Self-Selection**

Specifically, through the lens of vetting a board position (or any position, for that matter), Diana highlighted the importance of knowing yourself. First, your values, integrity, ethics, and beliefs must be compatible with the opportunity's. Second, seeking to understand your own skills, differentiators, market value, and contributions can help you articulate specifically why you are an asset to an organization or help you politely decline a position because you self-selected out based on your self-assessment. Being intentional, thoughtful, and consistent in understanding yourself empowers you to make a decision resulting in your personal success, potentially influencing the organization's success as well.

Gravitas Takeaway

You are where you are because of the choices, impacts, and experiences you have had. If you are offered or included in a great opportunity that may seem surreal, don't succumb to impostor syndrome. You are worthy and have earned this opportunity. Leverage why the opportunity has presented itself to you and the value you can have by bringing *who you are* and *what you have experienced* to the table—your gravitas has positively impacted others; continue to leverage its impacts through seizing great opportunities.

MONKEY WORK
Ted DeZabala, Chief Strategy, Innovation, and Technology Officer at Deloitte

*I*t was time for Deloitte's annual multipurpose meeting of partners, directors, and senior managers of the advisory business
for the firm. Deloitte is a global professional services firm that
provides a variety of services to clients, primarily in audit and
assurance, consulting, financial advisory, risk advisory, and tax and
legal. Ted DeZabala was responsible for delivering a presentation
on what innovation and strategy they would apply in the coming
year. Ted had been wearing a handful of hats within the advisory business at the time, including the position of chief strategy,
innovation, and technology officer for Deloitte's advisory practice.
He was also global leader of the cyber risk services practice and

the US national leader of managed services and products. His teams were directly responsible for an estimated $4 to 6 billion in annual revenue for the firm, and his focus for this meeting was on presenting some initiatives that he believed would propel the firm into high potential growth opportunities.

After nearly two and a half decades at the firm, Ted had established himself as a dependable leader who performed at the highest level regardless of circumstance. His tenure and reputation were both welcomed and feared; team members knew they could depend on him to lead innovation, profit, and success, but they also knew sometimes that meant change. Ted was in the top 5 percent of partners at the firm and the top 1 percent of leaders, both in performance and in position. He had strong relationships with the CEO and the firm's board members, and shortly before this annual multipurpose meeting, Deloitte leadership told Ted he was being considered for the advisory division's CEO position.

Ted began his presentation excited and confident, as he had hundreds of times before. After all, Ted had a strong reputation for his presentation skills and audience awareness. But this time, during a portion of his presentation where he was describing a function of the business that he anticipated would be drastically changed in the future due to technological innovations, he referred to some of the mundane functions of this division as "monkey work," trying to emphasize that even the most sophisticated teams have a requirement for mundane tasks. He knew that some of the team members within the audience were a part of this function of the business. Not thinking anything of it, he finished his presentation and walked back to his seat where he just so happened to be sitting next to the leader of the division he described as executing monkey work. She leaned over to Ted and said, "I don't know how we will recover from what you said. I have hundreds of texts and emails about what you just said." Ted immediately became curious about what she meant.

Following that meeting, Ted began to notice that there were two categories of people within the firm. The first category was people who came up to Ted and thanked him for referencing the division's functions that needed to be embraced by the firm due to technological innovations. The second were people who pointed out how hurt they were that Ted had referenced their service line and work as *monkey work*. In the weeks that followed, Ted was in the final stages for the promotion opportunity to become the advisory division's CEO. Ultimately, he did not receive the promotion. One of the primary pieces of feedback given to him by the selection committee partners and members was that he didn't have the respect of all the business units and divisions; they saw that as a critical dependency for whoever was to be CEO. Though disappointed in how two words had drastically changed the trajectory of Ted's future, he understood the realities of the consequences of his choice in words.

Ted continued accelerating growth and innovation in his existing role another five years until he retired. Reflecting on the event and effects it had on his career, many thoughts and reflections came to his mind—good and bad.

Ted's Takeaways

1. Words Matter

Ted's intent was not to dismiss the important (but mundane) functions of the business unit's work he referenced as "monkey work" or to label the work as unsophisticated. But that's how many team members received his communication. In the moment, Ted was oblivious to the mood of the audience, and when people shared immediate feedback with him, his first thought was, *How could you not understand what I was trying to point out?* Ted's lack of GAP in the moment and lack of intentionality behind his words could have been easily avoided if he'd had the self-awareness—the situational awareness—necessary to anticipate how his words might be received and identify how the audience was responding in real time with nonverbal cues and lack of positive engagement. He could have noticed it was in contrast with how his gravitas was traditionally received within the firm.

2. Adjusting Your Individual Brand and Reputation

In the weeks, months, and years that followed, Ted realized that throughout his first twenty-five years in the firm, he had established himself as a leader of specific teams or divisions instead of a leader of the organization, with the focus on success for the entire enterprise. The teams Ted had been a part of and led within Deloitte were commonly known as the best performing and most profitable functions of the business. But describing a function of a business unit as "monkey work" provided Ted's critics an opportunity to amplify the fact that he did not have appreciation or consideration for all parts of the business, just the highest-performing ones. It didn't matter whether this was true; his words made people *feel* a certain way and that affected his ability to win them over as his champions. His gravitas was affected.

This point brings up an interesting consideration for emerging leaders who are expected to drive performance in a specific department or team, sometimes even competing against other regional departments and teams within the organization. This may create a system where leaders are promoted based on their specific team's performance within the organization, but once they reach a certain level, they are graded on their track record of being a demonstrated leader of the *organization* and not just their *specific team*. This, more than ever, demonstrates a need for the GAP Enhancement Cycle so we can continuously evaluate how we are supporting both expectations.

3. Pride Can Be a Problem

Ted was leading the thoughts, anticipations, and possible solutions of strategy and innovation for the advisory division of Deloitte. His team was solving a problem they'd identified. This created a recipe for pride and ego to influence Ted's judgment on how his team's innovative solutions would be received by others within the organization. The solutions he and his team proposed had mostly been discussed, created, and vetted within his strategy team but not collaborated on with other divisions, departments, and teams within the organization. Ted shared, "This wasn't really about collaboration within the official structures of the firm. In fact, collaboration was necessarily extensive. It was about being an elitist. I was more collaborative with higher performing individuals and could be dismissive of those who didn't measure up. Many influential leaders fell into the latter category."

Gravitas Takeaway

Words matter and can have significant influence on your gravitas. Choose them wisely.

A SALE GONE WRONG
Joe Nunziata, Cofounder and CEO of FBC Mortgage, an Acrisure Company

*W*alking into the familiar boardroom, Joe and his brother Rob felt the difference this time; they were about to use specific protocol and procedures of *Robert's Rules of Order* to relieve the CEO of Sterne Agee and his son, the chief legal officer, from their positions and authorities within the company.

Joe Nunziata and Rob started FBC Mortgage in 2005. By 2011, they had received an offer from the Alabama-based investment banking firm, Sterne Agee, to purchase their company. After some preliminary discussions and due diligence by reputable accounting firms, Joe and Rob decided to accept the offer and they sold their company. As part of the acquisition, Joe and Rob stayed on to run FBC Mortgage for its parent company. After approximately a year with the company, Joe, Rob, and others from FBC became situationally aware of a handful of items that didn't seem right. More due diligence and awareness uncovered some unethical and possibly illegal activity by the CEO of Sterne Agee. Unsure whether anything was illegal but certain there were unethical practices taking place, Joe and Rob began to inquire with some of the board members (appointed by the CEO) whether the CEO was abiding by their fiduciary responsibilities. Once enough board members supported removing the CEO and his son for unethical and inappropriate handling of company funds, a board meeting was called to order. The CEO flew into the Orlando office of FBC on the company jet and was the last one to enter the boardroom, where he was met by a readied team. They executed the proper procedures, and effective immediately, the CEO and his son were relieved of their job titles and authorities. Joe handed the CEO a one-way ticket home on a commercial airline because he was no longer allowed to use the company jet.

Following the removal of the CEO and his son, the board needed someone to act as CEO who hadn't been skewed by the existing culture at the firm. After deliberating, the board selected Joe to help steer the company out of the hole it was in and toward a brighter future. Joe accepted and assumed the role of CEO. When he arrived at the corporate headquarters in Birmingham, Alabama, he learned several US government agencies wanted to seize and examine the firm's computers and equipment to look for evidence of wrongdoing. This made it quite challenging to begin a new chapter, but within a few years under new leadership, Sterne Agee became such an ethically functioning organization that it was purchased by the brokerage Stifel in 2015, and Joe's gravitas was influential in the Sterne Agee redefined reputation. That transaction allowed Joe and Rob to negotiate buying back their company, FBC Mortgage, from Sterne Agee and Stifel at market price. Joe and Rob became independent and private owners of FBC Mortgage again. They invested their fifteen years of experience in the industry and some tough lessons learned, growing FBC Mortgage to what it is today. In 2022, FBC Mortgage was sold to Acrisure, a fintech company employing more than sixteen thousand employees in twenty-one countries.

Joe's Takeaways

1. **You Can Never Have Enough Situational Awareness**

   Joe and Rob hired professionals to conduct due diligence on Sterne Agee when they were discussing a potential transaction. The professionals conducted their due diligence and reported there was nothing to be too suspicious about, but reflecting later, they recognized that while outsourcing due diligence to "experts" was a mature thing to do, it also bred complacency. If they had looked at specific information, such as Sterne Agee going through three CFOs (chief financial officers) in five years or how certain industry standard practices were forgone by Sterne Agee's leadership, they could have had better situational awareness and identified that the transaction might not be a good fit. The biggest takeaway on this topic: Don't exclusively outsource your situational awareness. While a third party can assist in mitigating blind spots, there is still value in seeking situational awareness through your own lens.

2. **Are You Working *On* the Business or *In* the Business?**

   As we've seen throughout these examples, gravitas can be influenced by many different actions and circumstances. One thing Joe mentioned was that he had the great opportunity to begin in the mortgage business at the lowest level and learn almost all functions of the business. Not only did this improve his humility but it also increased his gravitas as he steadily rose to become a well-known name in the industry. Joe said, "As the CEO of FBC, when I can speak competently to one of my entry-level team members about their specific roles and responsibilities from my own experience and not just from my educated knowledge, it gains some respect which I think contributes to one's gravitas." While working *on* the business is required by leaders of organizations, a gravitas builder includes the competence and humility to still work *in* the business when appropriate.

3. **Earn Your Spot on Your Team Every Day**

   The greatest accomplishments are made by teams, and it was clear that Joe recognized his success would not have been possible without great team members who contributed along the journey. Through the lens of self-awareness, each team player, and especially a leader, can reflect on whether they are providing value to the team and earning their spot on it every day. This self-accountability reflection can increase self-awareness and prioritize doing what is necessary to earn your spot on the team each day, ultimately contributing to enhanced gravitas among those you work with.

Gravitas Takeaway

A lack of awareness can negatively influence your gravitas.

"WE'RE MOVING THE COMPANY HEADQUARTERS"
Rabbi Rob Thomas, Founder and CEO of Team Cymru

R abbi Rob Thomas requested that his sixteen team members at Team Cymru's headquarters in the suburbs of Chicago, Illinois, attend an important meeting. This time, though, he asked them to bring their spouses with them. As team members and their spouses entered their office and gathered in their meeting room, everyone was filled with curiosity regarding what this could be about. Once everyone was assembled, Rabbi Rob began with one brief and powerful statement: "We are moving our corporate headquarters, and I would like to invite you all to come." Before Rabbi Rob could continue, a team member asked, "Where to?" Before he could ask more, Rabbi Rob removed his hoodie to reveal his Mickey Mouse T-shirt underneath. "We're going to Orlando, Florida!"

After an enlistment in the United States Navy and a period in the cyber commercial sector, Rabbi Rob had bootstrapped and formally started Team Cymru in 2005. Team Cymru is a cyber company whose mission is to save and improve lives by working with security teams around the world, enabling them to track and disrupt the most advanced bad actors and malevolent infrastructures. Both Rabbi Rob and his wife were born in Illinois; many of their family members still lived there, so it made sense to start their family and business there. Six years after starting the company, Rabbi Rob had grown the organization to employ thirty team members (or as he referred to them, thirty families). Sixteen of the families he employed lived in the Chicago area and worked from corporate headquarters—a building that had been broken into three separate times. Many employees had to commute close to an hour each way, and Illinois' economic circumstances were beginning to worsen. Rabbi Rob and his leadership team were always intentional about maintaining awareness of the environment and realities their team faced. Harsh winters, unfavorable taxes, rising crime, and an increasingly unfavorable business climate made him feel like the odds were stacked against Rabbi Rob and his team. So, he decided to be proactive and explore a new home for his company.

Rabbi Rob and a select group of leaders set out to find their next location. They considered Texas, North Dakota, South Dakota, Florida, and a few other states. Florida was the top contender. When they arrived in Orlando to investigate possibilities, Team Cymru was greeted by community leaders and others involved in the Orlando Economic Partnership. This partnership exposed Team Cymru leaders to many opportunities—for their business, for themselves, but most of all, for their team members and their families.

Methodical in his approach, Rabbi Rob first did due diligence on the location he was selecting to ensure it would be great for his team. After analysis, on-site assessments, and meetings with community leaders in various cities and states, Rabbi Rob decided to move Team Cymru's headquarters to Orlando, Florida. When Rabbi Rob shared the news with his team in their Illinois-based office, it was the first time they'd heard about it. Rabbi Rob told me, "I don't believe in pre-panic, and instead of my team members' minds wondering, I just wanted them to come to the meeting with no biases and ready to hear what, why, and how I made this decision."

Continuing his presentation in a Mickey Mouse T-shirt, Rabbi Rob shared a full overview of every thoughtful detail he and the leadership team took into account: business incentives, pattern of life considerations for team members, school system rankings, grocery stores, and so on. If there was a topic or category that Rabbi Rob thought might be important to one of his team members or their spouses, he ensured the information was included in his presentation. Finally, he said, "I would like to invite all of you to come with us. I will cover all of your and your family's travel expenses associated with the move, to the extent allowable by the IRS. Please think about it and let me know."

This was a big deal to Rabbi Rob. As a young company, assembling a team of thirty families, sixteen of which worked out of their current corporate headquarters, had not been easy; and having to potentially find replacements in Florida would be another challenging task. In the days following, Rabbi Rob heard from all sixteen families that they too were going to leave their extended family members in the Chicago area, leave the communities they had known and grown comfortable in, and move to Florida with Rabbi Rob. You read that right. All sixteen families committed to moving. During my interview with Rabbi Rob he said, "Seventeen of the sixteen families moved." Not understanding the numbers, I asked, "What do you mean?" He shared that a remote team member and his family who lived in Minnesota called Rabbi Rob when he got the news and asked if his family could move too. Rabbi Rob said yes, and seventeen families moved with him to establish their new corporate headquarters in Orlando, Florida.

Thirteen years later, all seventeen team members still work for Team Cymru, which has grown to employ 165 families and has increased their revenue twenty-five times. Rabbi Rob is still the CEO and occasionally wears his Mickey Mouse T-shirt.

I consider Rabbi Rob a very close friend and mentor of mine. I had to specifically ask him if I could interview him and include this story, because if it were up to him, he probably would have shared an example that was grounded in one of his failures. Knowing this story for years now, it was never a surprise to me that it happened. His gravitas inspired the kind of loyalty that caused his team to move cross-country for him without hesitation. For those who know Rabbi Rob, he is someone with an overly generous heart, an incredibly intellectual brain, and who regularly follows the GAP Enhancement Cycle to hold himself accountable to be the best leader he can be for his team members, community, and family.

Rabbi Rob's Takeaways

1. Never Assume You Have Gravitas Even If You Did the Day Before

When I told Rabbi Rob that I had always been impressed with his gravitas, he laughed. "Ah, I don't know. I never set out to have gravitas or to be a great leader, I'm just genuinely interested in people and want to be a good teammate."

Continuing my curiosity, I asked, "Well, what advice can you give to those who want to know how you've been so successful at what many would refer to as having gravitas?" Rabbi Rob said that one should never assume they have gravitas, even if they were confident they did the day before; this assists a leader in maintaining humility and self-awareness. People who have successfully gained a good

reputation or built strong gravitas in the category of leadership are those who have a significant amount of credibility.
Consistently do what you say you are going to do and excel
at it to get on the road toward developing strong gravitas.
As a quick tool, ask yourself where you fall on the "say/do"
ratio scale: *How much of what I say I will do, do I actually do?*
We're not perfect, but that scale matters when it comes to
enhancing your gravitas.

2. **Be Genuinely Interested in People Through
   Practiced Presence**

   When Rabbi Rob is interacting with another human being,
   he's interested. Not because a self-help book told him to
   be or because he's being strategic to build rapport with
   someone to get something he wants from them; he's interested because he truly believes he can learn something from
   everyone he interacts with. During our discussion, Rabbi
   Rob pointed out that so many people and leaders will advise
   others to be an active listener. And while he believes this
   is absolutely required, he equally believes it is important
   to engage in about 50 percent of the talking and sharing
   when you are interacting with another human being. He
   said, "What's the point in meeting someone for the first
   time and only asking them a bunch of questions only for
   them to leave that interaction thinking, *That was great, but I
   didn't learn anything about the other person?*" By sharing about
   yourself, your ideas, and your experiences, you are able to
   engage in two-way dialogue that shows the other that you
   are authentic, human, and have a story too. People don't
   want to follow a leader who is always reserved, closed off,
   and acts like a robot. They want to follow a leader who is
   human just like them.

3. **Know When to Be Serious and When Not to Be**

   Self-deprecating humor breaks barriers, displays humility,
   and, often, shows you are self-aware. Obviously there are

times to be serious and lead from an emotionally reserved position, but humor can assist team morale, especially when times are stressful or morale is down. Often overlooked, self-deprecating humor can show a human side to you that can win over trust and human connection, furthering your gravitas and your team members' willingness to follow you.

4. **Surprises Are Only Good During Hanukkah**

Through the lens of situational awareness, it is important to put yourself in others' shoes when you are leading them. By doing so, you can frequently ask yourself, *If I were a team member, would I want to be surprised by this?* Rabbi Rob asks himself this question because, "As a leader, my awareness usually tells me that imagination, assumption, and the unknown can sometimes lead to negative thoughts, behaviors, and responses. So, to keep my team members from being surprised, I leave the surprises for Hanukkah and not regularly occurring on the calendar. Communication is the primary vehicle to avoid surprises. 'News' is not good or bad news, it's just news. We interpret it and then classify it as good or bad, which emphasizes how important our transmitting and communicating is to others."

5. **Embody Your Mission**

If you want to create a culture so strong that when you decide to do something transformational—like move your corporate headquarters to another state and ask your entire team to go with you—you must have, above all, strong values and a mission your team knows you live by. "When we say our mission is to save and improve lives, we actually live by that, and we embody it with our actions every single day," said Rabbi Rob. As the leader of Team Cymru, Rabbi Rob has been challenged more than a dozen times to sacrifice in order to do the right thing and embody their mission. Often, those sacrifices were of profits. But, to Rabbi Rob, it was never in question, because all he had to do was ask himself, "What action is in best support of our mission?"

By personifying the company mission time after time, Rabbi Rob has shown his team members that he doesn't just *say* this stuff, he *lives* it. What could be more powerful than following an authentic leader who is true to the core and lives his mission every day? Gravitas is gained through consistency of actions aligned with beliefs, time and time again.

Semiannually for close to twenty years, Rabbi Rob has asked his team members to complete a brief culture assessment. The results are not anonymous but are viewed only by Rabbi Rob. This allows him to maintain what he describes as "connective tissue" between himself, at the top, and Team Cymru's most recently hired team members. Almost every time, team members have ranked mission, team, and culture as the top three reasons they want to be there. Although the benefits and compensation are competitive, they have never been among the top three reasons that team members choose to stay. You want to achieve gravitas? Embody your mission every single day through your actions.

6. Have True Friends

Authenticity, vulnerability, accountability, sanity, and so much more can come from having true and close friends, Rabbi Rob says—and not just the person who will tell you you're being an asshole, but people who will add value to your life and bring comfort and warmth to your heart. Often, true friends can assist in deepening your thoughts and perspectives, assisting in heightening your awareness.

Gravitas Takeaway

Living and embodying who you want to be through all your actions creates authenticity in your gravitas.

A SPEECH THAT CHANGED MY LIFE
Admiral William H. McRaven (US Navy, Retired)

Admiral William H. McRaven (retired) depicted here flashing the "Hook 'Em Horns" symbol to graduates after making the commencement keynote address at the flagship campus in Austin on May 17, 2014.
(AP Photo/ The University of Texas at Austin, Marsha Miller)

*A*dmiral William H. McRaven was readying to take the stage for a speech that, unknown to him at the time, would change his life forever. He was set to deliver the commencement speech to the University of Texas's graduating class of 2014. After thirty-seven years of military service, Admiral McRaven was getting ready to retire, and he saw this speech as another opportunity to transform the lives of thousands of young people before they would set out into the world and create their own legacy, with hopes of positively impacting as many people as possible along the way.

There are not many military leaders throughout the history of the United States who have accomplished and experienced as much as Admiral McRaven did throughout his career. Though, through his humility, he disapproves of me making this statement, I'll let you be the judge as I share just a few of his accomplishments. Retiring as a four-star admiral, William McRaven served as the ninth commander of the United States Special Operations Command (SOCOM) and, prior to that, commanded special operations forces at every level. His career included combat during Desert Storm and both the Iraq and Afghanistan wars. He commanded the troops that captured Saddam Hussein and rescued Captain Phillips. McRaven is also credited with developing the plan and leading the Osama bin Laden mission in 2011. After retiring from the military, and following his impactful commencement speech to the University of Texas, he became the chancellor of the University of Texas System where he led for three years. McRaven is a recognized international authority on US foreign policy and has advised Presidents George W. Bush, and Barack Obama, among other US leaders, on defense issues. He has authored more than half a dozen books. At the time of this writing, Admiral McRaven's commencement speech from 2014 has well over ten million views on YouTube. The speech also influenced his decision to author his #1 *New York Times* best-selling book, *Make Your Bed*, which as of this book's release has sold over one million copies throughout the world.

In addition to all his professional accomplishments, he has been married to his college sweetheart, Georgeann, for close to five decades.

Despite all his incredible accomplishments and credibility with some of the world's greatest leaders, when we connected for our interview for this book, he said to me, "Jacob, despite all I have done, when I meet people now, they know me as the guy who gave a speech and wrote a book on 'making your bed.' Most don't even know I was a SEAL or in the military."

So, what preparation went in to delivering a speech that would ultimately redefine Admiral McRaven's life and give him celebrity status among business leaders, politicians, and academics? Essentially, a lifetime of operating, learning, and growing in a GAP laboratory.

McRaven conducted his own root-cause analysis to identify where many of his GAP qualities began to appear, and that led him to his exposure and involvement in sports as a young child. From there, his life experiences tested, enhanced, and produced his own methodologies for regularly increasing his gravitas, awareness, and presence. To further understand some of what has forged McRaven's GAP, we'll jump right into his takeaways and reflections.

McRaven's Takeaways

1. Find Where You Were/Are Most Confident

When McRaven thought about where he first developed a sense of confidence and gravitas among others, his memory led him to playing pickup sports in his neighborhood growing up. He was more athletic than many of the kids in his neighborhood, which created an expectation for McRaven to be the all-time quarterback and play offense and defense in sports that required it, or anything else that meant he would be utilized to the max. As McRaven grew older, he continued to excel in sports among the kids in his neighborhood but also at his high school and with their rivals. As a track runner, McRaven set the school record for fastest mile, clocking in a 4:30 mile time.

As he went off to college at the University of Texas and began practicing with his new college team, he quickly recognized where the phrases "big fish, small pond" and "big pond, small fish" came from: He now had teammates much faster and more athletic than he was. During our discussion, he referenced that in 1973, some teammates of his could run under four-minute miles. It was here that McRaven remembers being humbled, which ultimately increased his self-awareness that outside of his small community, there are people who can perform better than he can.

Though humbled and leaving college with a heightened sense of awareness, McRaven also recognized that he could lean into his *confidence* as an athlete, and the skills he developed as an athlete, in all areas of his life. Sports set a foundation for McRaven's confidence in himself. That foundation of confidence allowed him to build off it through continuous exposures, learnings, and challenges.

His advice to leaders setting out to begin building their GAP is to "first, find *that thing* you are most confident doing and utilize that confidence to provide you with the courage to begin working on enhancing your GAP. You can build it, learn it, create it, and apply it at any time in your life, but if you go back to when you were young and find *that thing* that you were really good at…pull from that energy and confidence, and apply it to what you're doing today."

2. **Be Surrounded with Those Better Than You**
When McRaven first showed up to his first SEAL Team in 1977, he was immediately bombarded with questions, inquiries, and probes into his personal life. His veteran SEAL teammates were searching for vulnerabilities they could use to figuratively get under his skin and joke with/at him. This immediately exposed McRaven to an organizational culture where you had to be a regular practitioner of self-awareness, or your weaknesses and lack of self-awareness would be exposed and ultimately used against you.

Though this might be an extreme example, there are lessons to be drawn from it. Your environment matters. In the SEAL teams, there is always someone smarter, stronger, and faster than you. The environment you are in will continuously influence who you are and who you become. If you want to enhance your GAP, be intentional about who you associate yourself with and what environments you are in—they might just positively or negatively influence you. After leading at every level in the SEAL teams, McRaven gained confidence and awareness each time he elevated into a new position.

3. **Preparation, Preparation, Preparation**

Learnings come through the steps of preparation. Regardless of McRaven's tenure and accomplishments, he is a consistent practitioner of preparation, visualization, and practice. In preparing for his University of Texas commencement speech, he first began with asking the following questions to himself: *Who was my commencement speaker forty years ago, and what makes one memorable? What would I want to hear if I were twenty-two and graduating in today's world? How can I connect with everyone regardless of their understanding of the military?* His list of questions progressed, and with his self-reflections came learnings and awareness on stories, lessons, and wisdom he could share.

"I never give a speech that I don't spend at least an hour rehearsing. I have a binder with clear plastic sheets and my own techniques of preparation for each speech. I almost always write my speeches myself. This way, it's already easier for me to deliver because it's my words, my thoughts, my emphasis, and my meaning. Furthermore, when I am visualizing my speech delivery, I must see myself as a winner! I also visualize myself being successful even in the worst of cases. I visualize for good circumstances and bad, this way, I am prepared for unexpected outcomes as well."

With these sharings, McRaven reminds us that we are often postured for success or failure through our preparation. And despite the fact that many people know this, they often fail to create the time in their busy schedules to be intentional about doing it. If you want to deliver commanding gravitas, preparation is your first step in achieving it.

4. Have Confidence in *Your* Process

In addition to McRaven's shared wisdom and perspectives on the importance of preparation, he also shared something that was the first for me. As McRaven described his preparation methodologies, he shared that he has never once read a speech in its entirety to anyone for feedback before delivering it live. To be clear, this has never meant he doesn't ask for advice from his greatest adviser, his wife, Georgeann, on a specific sentence or section of the speech; he does that often. But as it pertains to delivering the speech in its final draft from beginning to end, he was clear that he has never asked for feedback in his life. When I asked why, he replied, "Sometimes humans have a tendency when they are asked for feedback to find areas to provide it, even if it is not necessary. And the idea of someone listening to a speech I just spent hours creating to then share their objective opinions could create an avenue for me losing confidence in my own work. And so, I bypass a full speech rehearsal in front of others. This probably wouldn't work for most people, and I don't advise people to do it this way, but I'm transparently sharing my way and what works for me." Whether or not this works for you, we can learn from him to do what works for us individually, even if it is unconventional.

5. Competence Is Confidence

Throughout McRaven's life, he has had countless opportunities to meet with, advise, and collaborate with some of the most important names and figures in the world. He described meeting President George W. Bush for the first time when he was a Navy SEAL captain: "I walked into the oval office, I was probably forty-six years old and had spent close to twenty-four years in the SEAL teams by then, and I had never met a president in person. I walked in and

wanted to look confident but also not starstruck. I needed
to look and appear confident because I was competent in
my knowledge of my profession and capabilities, and they
needed to know that. It's also important to note that confidence and humility need to be appropriately used, and you
need the confidence to say, 'No sir, I don't know that.'"

McRaven's reflection on his first interaction emphasizes the importance of having competence. Competence
will influence your confidence, and with an appropriate
balance of humility and confidence, your gravitas can be
well received by those you're interacting with.

Years later, when McRaven would plan and lead the
Osama bin Laden mission, the first helicopter that flew
into the mission to drop off the Navy SEAL operators
executing the mission would have a hard landing in the first
few moments of the mission. That's where this infamous
photo was captured of then-President Obama and his team
watching the mission unfold live in the situation room.

What many do not know is that in this moment, Admiral McRaven said something along the lines of, "Mr. President, we have amended the mission." When I asked McRaven what was going through his head and how he proceeded to respond in a calm and collected manner, he said, "Frankly, there was no need for me to be anxious because I knew the guys were okay. I knew I had a backup helicopter. The reason I could be calm was because we had planned this and rehearsed this so thoroughly."

In other words, McRaven was competent in his knowledge of his team, the planning they had executed, and the capabilities of his men to continue the mission despite what many perceived as a major obstacle. McRaven frequently makes the assertion, "If you can't do the little things right, you'll never be able to do the big things right." Admiral McRaven's awareness was optimized because he focused on knowing himself, his team, and the environment. His presence and gravitas were evoked through his awareness and received by President Obama and his team, ultimately increasing their confidence and trust in his words.

6. Your Family's Influence on Your GAP

One of Admiral McRaven's secret weapons for staying grounded, humble, and being able to receive authentic and sometimes blunt feedback comes from his family and those closest to him. Despite having a celebrity-status reputation, there were times throughout McRaven's career when he would meet the leader of a nation, and that night Georgeann would ask him to pick up milk on his way home. They keep him grounded. To his wife he is still "Bill," and to his kids he is still "Dad." The importance of utilizing one's family and trusted friends for consistent feedback is an awareness multiplier.

Gravitas Takeaway

Find your things that make you unique in your process, and if they work, leverage them to enhance your gravitas. Uniqueness can often be utilized as a positive differentiator.

LEADING AS THE YOUNGEST IN THE ROOM
Rod Fox, Founder and CEO of TigerRisk Partners

*I*n 1991, Rod Fox was promoted to regional vice president of
the reinsurance company EW Blanch. At twenty-eight, he
was going to be one of the youngest employees of the fifty that
comprised the prized Minnesota team. Most team members were
fifteen years his senior, more experienced, and had been his superiors at one time or another. The first thing Rod decided to do
was speak to the team so they could hear from him directly, so he
mustered all fifty team members to the office's largest conference
room and then opened the door and walked in.

Growing up, Rod had two parents who were, as he described,
"some of the hardest-working people" he'd ever known. Rod was
raised not knowing anything other than hard work and giving
everything his best. Entering the reinsurance business right out

of college, Rod carried a piece of paper in his pocket every single day with these hand-written words:

1. be super aggressive
2. be in great shape
3. never miss an opportunity
4. nobody works harder

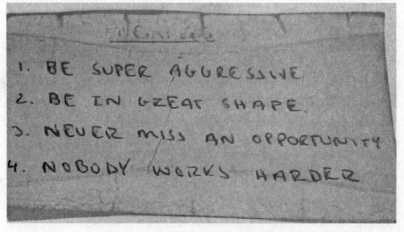

The hand-written note Rod kept in his pocket.

Following his own written advice, he quickly soared as a well-known team member, performer, and leader. Within six years, he was promoted to lead the top-performing division of the company, and a few years after that, Rod became the president of the company before taking it public. In the years to follow, Rod led and grew a few other reinsurance businesses and established a reputation as someone who radiated excellence and elevated those alongside him. In spring 2008, he and a close friend decided they were going to become entrepreneurs and do something on their own. Without an idea of exactly what they were going to do in the beginning, they received a call from a former Goldman Sachs CEO, then at a premier private equity firm, who wanted to meet with them. Rod and his partner met with the former Goldman Sachs executive and his team on Wall Street.

"I hear you two are planning to start something. Whatever it is, we want to invest $2 billion." The private equity firm hadn't seen a business plan or any indication of what Rod and his partner were going to start, but they weren't betting on the idea or business—they were investing in Rod and his partner. After establishing such a strong reputation in finance and insurance, Rod soon became certain that he wanted to do something without outside funding. So, in the wake of the 2008 financial crisis, Rod and his partner turned down the Wall Street offering of $2 billion in funding and started TigerRisk Reinsurance in Rod's living room with $2 million of their own money. Within a week, eight of the nation's top reinsurance brokers quit their jobs and joined TigerRisk. Again, not because of the company or its benefits but because of its leadership. After growing TigerRisk for fourteen years, the company's annual revenue was $250 million a year with more than 30 percent EBITDA (earnings before interest, taxes, depreciation, and amortization). In 2022, TigerRisk was acquired by Howden Insurance for $1.6 billion.

Rod's story provides a quick snapshot of the power of gravitas and reputation. During our interview, Rod made a point to share that gravitas is earned from your reputation and consistency of performance in one regard or another, whereas awareness and presence need to be continuously practiced, examined, and developed.

Going back to the moment of his first team meeting as a leader in Minnesota in 1991, before Rod entered the conference room to face his fifty colleagues, he used a technique that has always assisted him with developing his self-awareness. He began going through a mental checklist in his head: *What is important for the team to hear? What shows the team I am confident yet inclusive? Who will be my blockers and who will be my champions? If I were them, what would I want to hear? What judgments might some have of me that I can dispel in this moment? How do I communicate the vision of where we are going so everyone is excited?*

When Rod felt confident with the responses he had in his head to his own preparation questions, he left his office and walked toward the conference room. Before entering, a last reflection popped into Rod's head; he recalled words from the time he had the great fortune of hearing General Schwarzkopf speak: "When in command, take charge."

Upon entering, Rod quickly scanned the room to gain situational awareness by identifying the key team members he wanted to establish eye contact with during his delivery because he wanted to subtly challenge them, allow them to feel recognized, and gauge their body language to determine whether they were feeling apathetic or energized by his words. Well groomed, wearing a suit, and with two feet planted on the ground, Rod confidently and competently expressed his vision, his expectations of the team, and the direction he was hoping to take them. Rod received a positive response from the team. In his time as leader he delivered what he said he was going to deliver, and he never slowed down.

Speaking with me, Rod reflected on his career and thought it was important to share that moment in that conference room, primarily because he remembers that experience as pivotal in his journey in developing gravitas, awareness, and presence. He'd had enough experience at the time to have established a strong reputation, and with it, gravitas, which created a unique opportunity for him to continue his momentum despite being only twenty-eight years old.

Rod's Takeaways

1. Diversity Is a Performance Multiplier

How did Rod grow his awareness, maintain his presence, and become known for his gravitas? He credits his intentionality in gaining diverse knowledge, experience, and exposure. Rod never wanted to be known as just a great

reinsurance broker; he wanted to be known as a great businessman, leader, and team player. To be known as a great
businessman, he exposed himself to politics, sports, different
businesses, and other areas, seeking to answer the question,
What is happening in this domain? Then he followed up with
the question, *How is this relevant to the domains I function in?*
This way, Rod continuously gained situational awareness
of specific findings, social awareness of how people were
responding to industry-specific updates, and self-awareness
in reflecting on how he responded to the information. All
this awareness assisted him to become more valuable to
others regardless of the room he was in because of his depth
of knowledge. This created a mindset in Rod to always stay
diverse in what he was exposing himself to, who he was
building a network with, and what information he was
seeking to learn from. Rod said, "When you do a diversity
of things, it forces you to prioritize your presence and attention, which in return, often makes you more efficient with
your utilization in each domain."

2. **Credibility Through Performance Influences
   Gravitas**

   Sure, it's great to talk about a sense of gravitas and who
   comes to mind when we think of someone with gravitas, but
   if we conducted a root-cause analysis on why that person
   has gravitas, it most likely leads back to credibility. Being
   credible, dependable, trustworthy, and consistently delivering results can assist in creating gravitas with your team
   and those who know you. Internally, you are recognizing
   what you are capable of and gaining confidence through
   experience, success, resilience, and competence. All this can
   assist in building the confidence required to authentically
   exude gravitas, to the point where people don't just *think*
   you have gravitas, they believe it and count on it. If you are
   not known for performance and dependability or significant

accomplishments, it will be harder for team members and those around you to categorize you as someone with gravitas. In other words, hard work + doing it well = gravitas.

3. **Surround Yourself with GAP Practitioners**

Rod has never been a one-man show. He prioritized finding team members who had *passion*. He never cared if the passion was initially related to the work he and his teammates were doing; he just wanted to find people who, first and foremost, had passion for *something*. What usually comes with passion is commitment to be great in whatever category that passion exists. Therefore, Rod wanted team members who knew what it would take to accomplish something they were passionate about, often experiencing micro failures and having to overcome obstacles to achieve what they desired. Surrounding himself with people who had passion morphed into surrounding himself with people who would enhance his gravitas, awareness, and presence capabilities as he enhanced theirs.

Gravitas Takeaway

When one recognizes the power and influence that can come from consistently working on developing your GAP and putting in the hard work required to achieve it, great things happen.

CHAPTER 3

AWARENESS

The four types of awareness (SA4):

- ◆ Self-Awareness: The perception of self being aligned with the perception of others
- ◆ Situational Awareness: Understanding the context and details of an event or action
- ◆ Social Awareness: Understanding of the context and details of an exchange between two or more people, often determined by the environment
- ◆ Sensory Awareness: Understanding sensory responses (emotion, voice changes, body position, eye contact, etc.) to a situation or event

"OH SHIT, I WAS PROMOTED—OH SHIT, I MIGHT BE FIRED"
Robert Schleusner, Head of Wholesale Credit at Bank of America

R obert Schleusner had just been promoted to head of whole-sale credit for Bank of America. To put that into perspective, Robert's position ranked among the top thirty executives of the two-hundred-thousand organization. Of the $85 billion of revenue Bank of America earned annually, Robert and his new team of four thousand people were responsible for approximately $6 billion. Not to mention Robert's responsibilities of revenue and people spread across more than one hundred cities and more than twenty countries throughout the world. Within the first ninety days of taking this position, Robert tried to consume information as best he could. He scheduled meetings with close to one hundred leaders and relied on the proven formula that had made him successful: tight schedule, intense expectations, performance demands of his team, and no bullshit.

Six months after he'd been promoted, Robert looked around and realized that out of his four-thousand-person team, he would be lucky if one person chose to follow him any longer. He had an intense feeling that he had been doing something wrong, and if he did not fix it soon, he would be fired.

Born and raised in Alabama, Robert is tall with a Southern drawl and commanding presence when you're in a room with him. When it was time for Robert to decide where he wanted to start his career, he sought out New York, primarily because it exposed him to a world that was very different from Alabama. In 1991, he moved to New York City and began working at a trading desk for Lehman Brothers. After meeting his wife and finishing his executive MBA, Robert moved back South and established home base in North Carolina. It was there that he transitioned into the world of banking and was hired by NationsBank, acquired by Bank of America a year later in 1998. For eighteen years, Robert climbed the corporate ladder and established himself as a doer who would get done whatever was put in front of him. Operating in a capital markets group, Robert was a leader of a 150-person team for four years starting in 2011. In 2015, Bank of America decided to create a wholesale credit division that would essentially be a one-stop credit shop for businesses of all sizes and geographies: loans, credit cards, derivatives exposure accounts, retirement management for the employees, and so on. The leader of this division would be tasked with creating the division's culture, ensuring team alignment, eliminating inefficiencies, harmonizing processes, integrating new technology and data transformation, and a whole lot more. Robert was offered the position. He was excited for the opportunity to grow by doing something he had never done before, and he was pleased that the division would be in North Carolina. He would not need to be in New York four days out of every week and could spend more time with his family. Robert accepted.

But then, six months into the job, Robert became self-aware that he was failing. His initial instinct was to blame his problems on circumstances or other people. Taking time to reflect, he could not identify what he needed to do differently or better to turn his performance around. Self-aware that what he was doing was not working but still blind to how to fix it, he began to explore options for counsel. While thinking through his options, his wife came to mind as a potential source of feedback, but she didn't see him at work and was busy raising their children. He considered asking his peer colleagues and superiors, but he didn't feel right asking for their time, knowing they were just as busy as he was. So he began a thorough search for an executive coach. Robert worked with his coach on a regular basis. With full transparency, he gave his authentic thoughts and answers to questions during their sessions. Robert quickly began to identify some areas he could improve. Here is what Robert, with the help of his coach, identified he needed to change:

- *His leadership style*: He'd been exuding the kind of gravitas that made people see him as intense, determined, self-interested, and focused on transactional efficiencies. Though this style of leadership had worked for the past eighteen years, it wasn't going to work in the new leadership role that required him to build, assemble, implement, and align a massive team in a short amount of time. He needed to reorient his gravitas.

- *His self-limiting beliefs*: Throughout his career, Robert had developed experience bias that created an illusion of what *right* looked like to him. But formulas that had proven successful in the past were not applicable in the new position because the requirements were different, and he had to accept that. "My key self-limiting belief was that I needed to prove I was worthy of the seat I was occupying. I had impostor syndrome, and when I had a tough day, I felt unworthy as a person. That was causing me to show up in a transactional way, and I brought intensity to everything I touched. I wanted to prove that I belonged, and I was trying to force outcomes," he said.

- *His transactional take on relationships*: By design, the banking industry is transactional. The services, offerings, and solutions banks provide for their customers are transactional: You give me something, I give you something, and we finish. So, naturally, growing up in the financial services and banking industries, Robert's leadership style became very much like the system—transactional. Robert's meetings were scheduled so close together that not only did he have no time to think between them but he also didn't have time to build meaningful relationships with anyone he was engaging with. Unintentionally, he began to develop a reputation for not being interested in people's personal lives or building authentic relationships with those he worked closely with. True or not, people's perception is people's reality. "Relationships will drive performance. Without relationships, the performance will suffer, because while people will comply with what I want done, they won't commit and go the extra mile while using every resource they have to ensure a successful outcome," Robert said.

Doubling down on his efforts with his coach, Robert was intentional about turning the identified items around. He knew that by being intentional and following through his intentions with his actions, he would mitigate his existing blind spots, stretch himself in ways that would enable his success, and gain buy-in from team members who would willingly follow him. Over the next several years, Robert successfully transitioned from his singular leadership style to a dynamic leadership style unlike anything he had ever practiced before. He led and grew his team for six years before choosing to retire.

Robert's Takeaways

1. Gravitas Is Versatility

What will a scenario, role, position, or circumstance demand of your leadership style? Being aware of these requirements will allow you to develop the gravitas you know may be required of you. Or, like Robert, it will help you identify what areas you are not confident in and therefore will lead you to seek assistance from a coach or other team members. By simply *slowing down* and taking a step back, a leader can better understand the dynamics they must navigate, which will enhance their perspective. They can then make a prioritized decision of what to focus on and when.

It's important not to limit your leadership versatility. If there are opportunities within your organization or team to try new things or learn new components of the business without having to jump into the leadership role, take them. These opportunities will increase your self-awareness, specifically identifying what you're good at and where you need to develop. These opportunities will also increase your situational awareness, helping you better understand what departments or parts of the business are intertwined, dependent, or related to other parts of the business. Robert shared, "Through having situational awareness as just described, you will be able to gain valuable insight into and exposure to what's required to influence people outside your organization. I see many leaders who have one go-to move, and that doesn't work for them as they continue to progress in their careers and leadership responsibilities."

Finally, by looking through the lens of social and sensory awareness, you can gain appreciation for the personalities and characteristics of team members. You can notice if a certain type of personality is more common in a specific department of your organization, or if you don't usually interact with a certain group and need to get to know them better. All these things combined will assist in developing your gravitas and awareness, ultimately making you a more versatile leader.

2. You Need to Schedule Awareness

When Robert hired his executive leadership coach, he quickly realized that he lacked thorough and consistent awareness. He hadn't had time to intentionally think about his self-, situational, social, or sensory awareness. Before working with his executive leadership coach, Robert described his state of being as "busy" instead of "intentional." Robert told himself that he was too busy and didn't have time for these things; but the reality is, we all make time for what we want. It may sound crazy, but the reality is, if your typical workday is jammed with sixteen back-to-back meetings and you don't schedule the time to think, time will fly and you may not reflect on yourself or your actions for months, maybe years. This is why so many executives are a part of the 5 a.m. club: They get up at 5:00 a.m. to guarantee themselves an hour of strategic thinking, reflection, or creativity before their workday begins (which is often difficult if you're leading teams in multiple time zones). Consistently making the time to reflect and think strategically won't just assist you in being a great leader of yourself and others but will also assist in enhancing your GAP.

Robert knew his relationships were transactional. The mindset of "this is what is required to operate at this level" might sometimes be true, but not all the time. Robert gained appreciation for the value and impact awareness could have on his relationships and the business. Intentionally allocating more time for meetings empowered Robert to use a portion of his time to engage in personal relationship-building discussions with his team members; celebrating team successes and checking in with his team members' well-being became standard. This assisted him in fostering meaningful relationships that made team members *want* to work for him and follow him. Robert described this change in his team members as shifting from *compliance* to *commitment*.

3. If You're Not Humble, Chances Are You Won't Increase Your Awareness

Robert was convinced that he would have been fired or replaced if he did not fix what he had self-identified as not working. Or, more important to him, he wouldn't have made progress that influenced his team in a positive way. You need humility to be open to exploring your lack of awareness. Robert was a top executive at an $85 billion organization. Despite his tenure, status, and title, he did not allow those things to sabotage his humility or prevent him from raising his hand when he needed help, especially when it came to working on himself. He had to ask himself a few key questions that we all should consider: *Am I willing to be honest with where I am and ask hard questions? Is the way I've been showing up still serving me? Am I open to alternative perspectives? Am I willing to change?*

Awareness Takeaway

Intentionality is a critical part of awareness, and if not consistently practiced, it could have significant negative impacts.

SOVIET COUNTERINTELLIGENCE MEETS THE BEAUTY INDUSTRY
Jennifer Walsh, Founder of Beauty Bar

J ennifer was going into her eighth meeting with one of the most powerful businessmen in the food franchising industry. Thirty-year-old Jennifer Walsh, a new entrepreneur, had considered every meeting and interaction with him an incredible opportunity to soak up as much knowledge, insight, and wisdom as she could. But this meeting did not turn out as she had expected.

In 1998, Jennifer Walsh founded Beauty Bar, a first-of-its-kind retail store that included dozens of beauty products from different companies—who were small, large, and everything in between—under one roof. She had a weekly television segment in which she described the ingredients, origin, and value of small beauty product companies compared to well-known national brands. This inspired her to create a concept unlike anything else before. Beauty Bar was the first retail store in the United States to include biophilic design (living plants, water fountains, exposed wood, green walls, etc.) in their retail space and one of the first to offer curbside pickup for their products. Beauty Bar also carried skin care products for men and regularly had social gatherings at their stores where customers could enjoy drinks while they shopped (or while waiting for someone shopping). These concepts were revolutionary in 1998, and after Jennifer opened her first store in Neptune Beach, Florida, she received a lot of attention for the disruption she was pioneering in the beauty industry.

As the attention and her enthusiasm took the industry by storm, Jennifer heard from one of the most powerful and influential businessmen in the food franchising industry; we'll call him "Henry." Henry was a trailblazer of his own who had founded and grown two independent food franchises to international fame and that still prosper today. He established a reputation as someone who was successful at anything he did. So, when he reached out to connect with Jennifer, she saw it as a tremendous opportunity for learning and mentorship. During Jennifer's first meeting with Henry, she tried to absorb as much as she could from his wisdom and experience, and they quickly set a plan to meet regularly for the next three months. Jennifer shared that Henry's gravitas both from his reputation and how he filled the space of the environment commanded respect.

In the late nineties, young female business owners were extremely rare. Most beauty brands were led by male business executives. Jennifer recalled that shortly after opening her first location, a female shopper asked Jennifer what her husband did for work. When Jennifer replied, "I'm not married," the woman asked, "Well, how can you have all of this?" Our society has made some progress in the last twenty-some years, but the unique contexts and obstacles Jennifer faced at the time were quite overwhelming. Recognizing she needed a trustworthy champion for detached wisdom, she leaned on her dad. Her father had just retired after twenty years as an FBI agent specializing in counterintelligence. Throughout his career, he had to be on top of his game to successfully beat the Soviet Union at the tradecraft they were frequently credited with creating. So, when Jennifer called to debrief her first meeting with Henry, her dad asked her some specific questions to heighten her awareness of the interaction: *How did he speak to you when he first met you? What was his body language like? Were there specific topics he seemed adamant to cover? Did anything feel "off"?* Jennifer reflected on these questions and couldn't identify anything out of the norm, but they increased her awareness, presence, and alertness for her next meeting.

Following her second connection with Henry, she called her dad again. "Dad, he kept asking for information and specifics on my financials and our financial performance." Her dad replied, "Don't ever feel like you have to share anything you don't want to share. And it can be beneficial to not divulge all the information about your business." Jennifer took this as sound advice and reassurance that she did not have to disclose information she deemed confidential.

When Jennifer connected with Henry for their eighth meeting, he demanded she share with him Beauty Bar's financial performance. When she declined, Henry stared her in the eyes and said, "I want you to know I am planning on opening a similar but better concept than yours right down the street. You can join me and be a part of this or I will make it a priority to crush you." Jennifer gave him a look that said, *Bring it!* and left.

While debriefing with her father and reflecting on her interactions with Henry, she realized he'd had malicious intentions from the very beginning. If it were not for her father's wisdom earned from years of reading and understanding people, she may have provided Henry with proprietary information leading to Beauty

Bar's downfall. Henry opened a competing concept down the street a few months later, but Jennifer believed in herself, her work ethic, her competence, and the brand she represented. Jennifer was determined to succeed despite the competition, and she did. Henry had to close his location within a year of opening. Over the next ten years, Jennifer grew Beauty Bar into five locations with more than one hundred employees throughout Florida and eventually sold the company to Quidsi, who almost immediately sold it to Amazon. None of this would have happened if Jennifer hadn't invested in self-awareness, situational awareness, sensory awareness, and social awareness in her interactions with Henry.

Jennifer's Takeaways

1. **"It Gave Me Confidence and Increased My Vigilance"**

   Jennifer reflected on her initial interactions with Henry and said that her mindset at the time had been positive. Though their relationship had grown into something challenging and terrifying at the time, she grew exponentially from that experience. It boosted her confidence to know that someone with substantial credibility had taken an interest in her innovative idea and was so enthusiastic about it that he wanted to own it. It heightened her vigilance because she realized people often have an agenda for a personal outcome, and while that isn't necessarily a bad thing, it is something to be aware of when someone takes a unique liking to you and your ideas or when you're on your way to success.

2. **Age Does Not Determine Competence or Capability**

   Henry thought because of his resources, gravitas, and network he would be able to, as he put it, "crush" Jennifer and her Beauty Bar. But Jennifer just doubled down on what had made her successful up until that point—grit, determination, and ensuring she was the most knowledgeable person on relevant topics at the table. Jennifer thinks Henry felt he could bully her because she was a woman and a new entrepreneur, but mostly because she was young and inexperienced at business. What Henry did not account for was Jennifer's commitment and belief in her brand, the brands she represented in her stores, and the passion she had for the transformation she was creating in the beauty industry. Jennifer said, "Just because you're young does not mean you cannot be the most competent and capable. Those two things are in your control."

3. **Be Aware of How People Speak to You When You First Meet**

   What is the biggest piece of advice Jennifer's ex-FBI agent father shared with her that she says still holds true today, almost thirty years later? If you are hyperaware of how someone speaks to you when you first meet, you can gather critical information that could provide greater findings the more you get to know and interact with them. How people engage with others the first time they meet says a lot about their intentions, values, priorities, and motives. To do this well, the four components of awareness need to be fully engaged: self-, sensory, situational, and social.

Awareness Takeaway

Jennifer managed to see past the influence of Henry's gravitas using advanced awareness techniques, and that led to the growth of her own. It's a reminder that growth in one area is an opportunity to strengthen and balance all three.

TIME-SENSITIVE TRANSFORMATION
Chris Brown, USA Women's Olympic Rugby Team Head Coach

New-Zealand born Chris had just been named the head coach for the USA women's Olympic rugby team. He was tasked with one mission: Help the women's team qualify for the next Olympic Games.

Until then, Chris had been an assistant rugby coach for more than a decade, working with teams in South Africa, Kenya, and Namibia. Before accepting the head coach position of the USA women's team, he had been the assistant coach for the USA men's Olympic rugby team for four years. During that time, he was physically located with the team in San Diego, California, whereas the head coach was based in London and commuted to California for long stretches of practice and matches. Because Chris was the second in command of the men's team and lived where the team did, the players confided in him and sought his council beyond the rugby field. In just twelve months after Chris and the head coach took over the men's program, they turned around their team's culture. They ranked sixth in the world and won their last world series tournament of the season, two things that the team had never done before.

In 2018, the men's team went on a three-month international tour, but complications with Chris's immigration green card meant he was unable to join them; he had to stay in the US. To continue providing value where he could, Chris and the organization saw the opportunity for him to support the USA women's rugby team for those three months. At the time, the women's rugby series had seven good teams and the USA women's team was consistently ranking fifth or sixth in the world. But Chris saw so much potential while working with them. Chris thought, *If we can just transform the culture and assist these players in believing in each other, they could be winners.* Chris felt the team had many toxic traits, including unhealthy competition with one another, lack of trust, and team misalignment.

Through Chris's direct efforts and three months of coaching, the players and team staff began to build better trust, rapport, and camaraderie between themselves and with Chris and their organization. One veteran player stated, "Wow, I really think we can be the best in the world if Chris coaches us." The women's team had known of Chris over the four years he'd been with the men's team because they trained at the same location, used the same facilities, and often collaborated on select events. Though they'd been familiar with him, this was the first time they were direct beneficiaries of his coaching and methodologies to produce a strong and culturally aligned team. The women's team players saw what Chris was able to do in a short time with the men's team, and they wanted him to do it with them, to help them win.

When Chris accepted the position as the head coach of the USA women's Olympic rugby team, he inherited four peers in management, twenty-five players, and a losing culture. This was the moment Chris had been waiting for for more than ten years; he was finally the head coach of a prestigious rugby team.

In the first four months, Chris struggled to influence the team in the way he had so many times before with the USA men's team and with teams in Kenya and South Africa. This was the first time he had formally coached a women's team—and his coaching style was not working as fast as he was used to. During a training period, the women's team was invited to compete in an invitational, and Chris saw it as a good opportunity to delegate his newly hired assistant coach to lead a subsegment of the players. Seeing a group of his players being coached by someone else would provide Chris with objective insights he could witness from the sidelines rather than the field. This act of delegation, empowerment, and observation changed the team's trajectory forever.

On the sidelines, Chris observed that his assistant coach, who had only been with the team for only five weeks, was really resonating with the players. They were listening, collaborating, and then acting like a unified team. While debriefing after the invitational, Chris realized that his assistant coach was providing positive reinforcement to the team and to individual players, emphasizing what they were doing right before sharing suggestions on how they could do better. Previously, Chris had focused on where the team and players could improve. Driving home that evening, Chris realized he was not coaching the players how he *wanted* to be coaching. After further reflection, he decided to change his style, technique, and approach. "If I want them to change, I need to change," he said.

A week later, Chris called a team meeting with the players and staff. He pointed out that he had realized he'd not been coaching to the best of his ability. He said that his assistant coach had shown through his actions that Chris could coach better. Reflecting on this, Chris shared with me that he was lacking situational awareness on how the players needed to be coached, and he hadn't picked up on social and sensory awareness responses from the players when he was coaching them. This skewed his ability to be self-aware. Though he didn't know it at the time, Chris was putting the GAP Enhancement Cycle into use, gaining real feedback from his self-evaluation and putting it back into an experiment. His humility at that team meeting changed the course of the next eight months in what I like to call *a purposeful pivot*.

After Chris's purposeful pivot with his team, they went on to win the next twenty-seven out of thirty matches, beating the current Olympic champions three out of four times and the world champions two out of three times. The USA women's Olympic rugby team finished their twelve-month stretch ranked second in the world, and six weeks after that they became the number one ranked team in the world. As Chris recounted this transformative story with me, he smiled sharing this last bit of information. "Our team was ranked number one in the world, but not a single one of our players were ranked in the top five of their respective positions. We were a team, not individuals."

Chris's Takeaways

1. **What Got You Here Won't Always Get You There**

   Chris had a demonstrated track record spanning a ten-year period of transforming teams into winning teams. Within the first four months of his head coaching position with the women's team, he realized that his coaching experience, techniques, and approaches that worked for him in the past wouldn't work with this team. These players were different in so many ways. If he tried to force his proven ways of coaching on the players and continued to identify *them* as the ones who were not able to change, he may not have had a breakthrough. Thoughtful reflection and evaluation made him more situationally aware and self-aware. In turn, that allowed him to adapt his coaching style to the needs of the team.

2. **Intention Requires Action or You Won't Get Results**

   Chris had intentions to turn the team around every single day he showed up to coach. But without thoughtful actions following through on his intentions, they would be meaningless. He told me, "I was not coaching how I wanted to coach." We see this occasionally with people who take on new leadership roles. In anticipation of being promoted to a leadership role, people often idealize how they will lead and what they will do to make themselves a great and admired leader. But when they receive the promotion, they become misaligned with how they wanted to lead. Why and how could this happen? They lack self-, situational, sensory, and social awareness.

3. **Purposeful Pivots**

   If Chris had just decided to change his coaching style without making an overt point to his team, it may have been overlooked. But Chris was purposeful in sharing his self-reflections and observations, and how he wanted to be better going forward. That meeting provided a platform for everyone to observe his intentional actions. He wanted to show he was serious. The value of purposeful pivots is that they let you reset the score card and make your team aware of new direction and expectations so they can hold you accountable and keep a close eye on your promised "change" moving forward.

Awareness Takeaway

Humility enables awareness. Action enables change.

SHATTERING MY PERFECT WORLD
Jeff Boyer, Vice President of Global Vehicle Safety at GM

Jeff was a rising star at General Motors (GM). Both he and his wife, Karen, were engineers at GM and had alternated going to graduate school to obtain their MBAs to advance into leadership at the company. Jeff became an executive in the 1990s and was quickly developing a reputation among his peers as someone others wanted on their team. After building their house together, Jeff and Karen moved in with their three boys and were living the life they dreamed of. But the same year they moved into their new home, Karen was diagnosed with lupus—an autoimmune disease that was chronic but manageable at the time. However, it quickly progressed, and they realized that Karen's lupus wasn't chronic but critical; a few months later, Karen suffered a cardiac arrest and ultimately passed away. From a rising executive at GM with a happy family to a single parent, Jeff's perfect world shattered in an instant.

Anyone who knows Jeff knows that he has always had an unwavering understanding of his values or, as he identifies them, his "true north." Reflecting on this emotional experience and what his family had gone through, he shared the importance of knowing oneself prior to facing difficult circumstances. By knowing yourself, you gain the confidence in what you are capable of, you identify where you need support from others, and you gain competence in knowing what wrong looks like, enabling you to identify what right *may* look like. When Karen passed, one of his first thoughts was, *If Karen were here, what would be her first priority?* As soon as he

Jeff and his three grown sons.

asked himself that question, a subtle smile spread across his face. He knew her first priority was raising the boys to be great people. After recognizing that, Jeff made a commitment to himself that no matter what *forward* looked like, his priority was going to be to raise the boys to be great human beings—because he was their dad and because it's what Karen would have prioritized.

It had been twenty-three years since Karen passed when I interviewed Jeff, and he recalled the lessons, wisdom, and take-aways he had gained from that experience. In the years following Karen's death, Jeff continued to accelerate within GM with the help of family, community, great leaders, and Dianne, who became his wife. Jeff navigated a difficult circumstance through awareness and strong relationships. Ultimately retiring as the global vice president of safety at GM, Jeff raised three incredible boys and is living in his perfect world again, side by side with his best friend and wife, Dianne.

Jeff with his three boys and his second wife, Dianne.

Jeff's Takeaways

1. Identifying Your True North (Self-Awareness)

Through Jeff's upbringing and interest in team-based sports, he'd identified his values from a very young age. He never placed them in a box of completeness but continuously revisited and evaluated his personal values. This gave him a sense of knowing himself, or self-awareness. He continuously asked himself, *Who am I? What type of person do I want to be? What do I want to be known for? What's important to me?* These questions helped him identify his values as positivity, integrity, and excellence. Those three values allow him to maintain his true north regardless of difficult situations, circumstances, or decisions. Though much of this book focuses on the importance of GAP in a professional sense, Jeff's story highlights the importance of GAP in a personal sense too. Because Jeff had a deep understanding of who he was, what was important to him, and what he stood for, he could focus his presence on navigating circumstances to the best of his ability, knowing what *right* looked like to him and his family. Jeff made sure to tell me, "People can endure any *what* if they have a strong understanding of their *why*." Many times, people will try to articulate their values based on society's standards of values, but this only creates a lack of self-awareness because it's not authentic. When you take the time to consciously think about the values *you* want to live by, you can make decisions that bring you a more purposeful life. Your values and self-awareness can influence your actions and intentions in everything you do.

2. Living with Intention (Situational Awareness)

Reflecting on what was, at the time, his "perfect world," Jeff admitted he was almost in some sort of trance at the time. He thought that because he was having a wonderful experience in life, it was the same for others. After Karen's death, he quickly gained appreciation for the reality that life is hard—and although losing Karen was one of the hardest things he had ever endured, many people face much harder realities and circumstances. Jeff and his family's experience forever changed who he was as a leader and as a person. From then on, his interactions with others changed—he began to lead by trying to be a great listener and expressing empathy and sympathy because he knew that everyone had their own challenges. In business and in life, people are quick to focus on the task at hand and the outcomes desired because that's why they have a job—to get things done. But situational awareness helps us understand and appreciate that fellow teammates, community members, and friends are also going through their own challenges outside of work. That assisted Jeff in establishing a reputation for being an empathetic leader. Remembering Karen as someone who brought positivity to all she connected with (more than eight hundred people attended her funeral), Jeff lives each day with intention, aware of how he is living each moment of his life. Jeff said, "We don't get to choose how long we have, but we do get to decide what we do with the time we have."

3. **Importance of Relationships (Social and Sensory Awareness)**

There was no way Jeff was able to pull through his family's circumstance without the assistance of his family, friends, leaders at work, and community. When Karen passed away, relationships Karen and Jeff had fostered for years paid off as people rallied to support Jeff as a new single dad. Carpooling, afterschool activities, and meals were just a few examples of where people stepped in to support their new family dynamics. Jeff's leaders at GM knew he needed to be home by 6:00 p.m. every night, so they intentionally supported his schedule with flexible hours and demands that would afford Jeff the ability to be home each night to provide some stability and consistency with his boys. Jeff and

Karen were intentional about building strong relationships with people, in all areas of their lives. This required intentional actions and thoughtfulness, but it was reciprocated when their family needed help from these relationships. If you are not intentionally creating meaningful relationships, if you're not thoughtful and aware of your social surroundings, relationships can be impacted.

Awareness Takeaway

Jeff's awareness on every level served as a firm foundation for his career and family life. It can do the same for us if we prioritize it.

WHEN YOU BECOME AWARE, ACT!
Lauren Crandall, Three-Time Team USA Field
Hockey Olympian and Team Captain

*L*auren took a sip of beer and shook her head in disbelief as she listened to her teammates debrief what had just happened and how things went wrong. It was two weeks after they'd arrived home from the 2012 London Olympic Games. The team she had captained finished dead last. She could not believe that was her reality and was determined to never experience it again.

Finishing anywhere but in first place was rare for the field hockey teams Lauren had been a part of her entire life. In high school, her team won the state championship. When Lauren attended Wake Forest, she and her team won two national championships, two conference championships, and lost just five matches in her four-year tenure. During her sophomore year in college in 2005, Lauren was awarded a spot on Team USA's field hockey crew, and she made the Olympic team. She competed in the 2008, 2012, and 2016 Olympic Games. In both 2012 and 2016, she was the team captain. As a giant and legend in the sport, she was inducted into the USA Field Hockey Hall of Fame in 2022.

In 2011, Team USA Field Hockey was preparing to compete in the Pan American Games. Lauren was team captain for the first time, and just weeks before, three former Olympic players became ineligible to compete due to injuries and for personal reasons. Pulling from their roster of twenty-four athletes, the team selected the next three best athletes to take their places. The three athletes were players newer to the team and had not competed in an Olympics. This created an ambiguous team anatomy shortly before competing. As underdogs and ranked thirteenth in the world, Team USA had to beat the second-best team in the world, Argentina, to advance to the 2012 Olympics—only the top twelve teams could compete. Through fierce competition, Team USA upset the world's expectations and advanced to the 2012 London Olympics with Lauren as team captain.

Five months later, the team was just four months away from the Olympic Games. Their three veteran Olympic teammates had returned to the team roster, and sixteen athletes were selected to represent Team USA in the Olympics. Lauren was again the captain of this team. Part of the team's intensive work was frequent training with a world-class sports psychologist. His methodology was to train the athletes to better understand themselves, their surroundings, their energy levels, and their presence. Since the Pan American Games, the sports psychologist had focused on individual awareness. As they geared up to begin pivoting to

team-focused awareness, the team's psychologist introduced facilitated debriefs after each practice.

In one particular after-practice debrief, the psychologist
probed for transparency and for players to comment on areas
where they believed the team could be doing better. One of the
star players on the team said, "I don't believe we are connecting
like we need to be; there is something missing, but I know we'll get
there." The team freely exchanged thoughts immediately following
the star player's comment, but at the time, Lauren didn't think too
deeply about it.

Just two weeks before the Olympics in London, the team rented
a farmhouse in the countryside of the United Kingdom to detach
from the Olympic Village and mentally prepare for the tough
matches ahead. The sports psychologist requested that each player
write a letter to the team and then had them gather in the farmhouse's common room to read their letters out loud. As letters were
read, Lauren heard many of her teammates mention the belief
and hope that they would medal at the Olympics. Lauren did not
include that in her letter, primarily because it wasn't something
anyone had ever said before—not in practice, not leading up to the
games, not in a debrief, and not at informal team events. Though
obvious that every Olympian's dream was to medal, Lauren too
assumed that was a goal but also wondered, *Why is this only being
discussed and visualized now? Why not before?*

Team USA won one match, tied one, and lost four in the 2012
Olympic Games, ultimately finishing in last place.

When the team returned to the United States, they had a team
debrief over a conference line. Following the debrief and after
identifying some needed changes, the team's coaching staff was
replaced by the deciding Olympic committees, and Team USA
set their sights on getting ready for the 2016 Olympics. Lauren
was voted team captain again by her peers, and through the new
coach's transformational leadership style, Lauren thought about
things she believed the team had done wrong leading up to the

2012 Olympics. She was determined to change the course of the team, and that she did.

Lauren's Takeaways

1. **When You Become Aware, Act!**

   Lauren often speaks about her greatest regret as team captain for the 2012 Olympics. When the star player said at their debrief, "I don't believe we are connecting like we need to be; there is something missing, but I know we'll get there," the players went on with their debrief. They were lacking situational awareness. The star player was signaling that she did not believe the team was synchronized on and off the field. Although many of the athletes may have felt it, no one said anything or tried a root-cause analysis of sorts to figure out what the team needed to do to reconnect, instead of just leaving it to "I know we'll get there." Lauren shared that if she could go back in time and change her response to that comment, she believes the team would have had a better shot to medal. This emphasizes the importance of being present yourself in order to be situationally aware of your environment.

2. **Situational Awareness Is Not a Hypothetical**

   Throughout the team's training regime, their expert trainers, coaches, psychologists, and other support would always share thoughts about where the team should be ranked based on their team's anatomy—individual talents and individual statistics—rather than focusing on where they were actually positioned in the global rankings. Furthermore, during team debriefs, their support specialists shared what actions were needed for the team to be winners in the next match. Lauren said this created an ecosystem where the athletes gave attention to hypotheticals shared with them by their support staff rather than prioritize the facts and performance metrics. Situational awareness describes current realities, not hypothetical ones. And success relies on our reaction to and awareness of current realities.

3. **GAP Requires Intentionality Paired with Action**

   Following the hard-to-swallow defeat experienced by Team USA in 2012, Lauren committed to doing better in the 2016 Olympics. She shared that she would not have identified some of the areas that went wrong if she had stopped competing after the 2012 Games. She needed to get back on the field and be intentional with her and her teammate's actions in order to do better at their next opportunity. In 2012, the team's intention was to perform well, but they did not follow through with their actions and came in last. Lauren led the 2016 Olympic team to a resilient fifth-place finish by being intentional—on and off the field—with the team's actions and about every element of their sport along the way.

Awareness Takeaway

Sometimes awareness can assist in identifying an opportunity that requires you and your team to slow down before speeding up. If awareness is not consistently practiced, you could miss a critical detail that might just be the difference between success and failure.

AWARENESS FOR SURVIVAL
Jessica Buchanan, Humanitarian and Hostage Rescued by SEAL Team Six

On October 25, 2011, Jessica Buchanan was taken hostage by Somali kidnappers while working as the education adviser for a nongovernmental organization. Abducted at gunpoint and held ninety-three days for ransom, the thirty-two-year-old woman was starved, forced to live outdoors in deplorable conditions, and terrorized by more than two dozen kidnappers. As Jessica's health steadily deteriorated, President Obama initiated an order for SEAL Team Six to rescue Jessica on January 25, 2012. Jessica was rescued and quickly began living her second chance at life to the fullest.

I connected with Jessica for the first time on a podcast four years before writing this book, and I took so much away from our conversation then.[43] When writing this book and thinking of practitioners who would provide unparalleled contributions on the topics of gravitas, awareness, and presence, Jessica came to mind.

On the podcast, she had discussed the type of self- and situational hyperawareness she was able to achieve in captivity, and I wanted to hear more.

Being a hostage is unimaginable for anyone. Jessica had gone through kidnapping trainings in a classroom and simulated practical exercises in the field, but nothing could have prepared her for the real thing. Being hostage for ninety-three days means 2,232 hours—a lot of time to do…nothing. Research on hostage stories shows that many at least have the opportunity to write on their prison wall or in a journal, read a book, or speak with someone in their native language.[44] Not Jessica. During her time in captivity, she had nothing. Separated from Paul, the Danish colleague who was also taken hostage by these kidnappers, Jessica was placed under a bush in a remote desert with nothing for miles around, exposed to the elements and under constant guard, while the kidnappers attempted to negotiate for a ransom in exchange for Jessica and Paul.

After the first couple of weeks, Jessica realized the situation was not going to resolve quickly and that she'd better come to terms with that. Jessica thought, *If I make it out of here alive, there are two things I'll probably never have again that are unique to this situation: (1) this much time doing nothing and (2) being in an environment that is so simplistic–sit here, wait, and again, do nothing.* Always an opportunist, she said, "This was my chance to do some deep work and find myself. So, I went back to my very first memory I could recall of my mom taking me to the movie theater for the first time, and I focused on the micro details of every single thing I could remember: the clothes she wore, the lipstick she had on, the way her teeth looked when she smiled, the taste of the coke and smell of the popcorn…" Jessica revisited neuro pathways she had not visited in such detail her entire life. Her mother had passed away unexpectedly about a year before Jessica was taken hostage, and she had not done any reflecting or self-talk in order to gain closure. Jumping from memory to memory and detail to detail,

Jessica methodically went through every single memory she had of important events, exchanges, and relationships with people. In doing so, she dealt with trauma, grudges, hard memories, and good memories. At thirty-two years old, she concluded her reflections with amplified awareness of her journey, what defined her, who she had been, who she was currently, and if she ever made it out of there, who she wanted to be. Filled with gratitude, she recognized the great life she had lived so far and felt an overwhelming sense of fulfillment.

When she couldn't think of any more memories to explore, she transitioned to dreaming and planning her future—if, of course, she were to make it out alive. During my interview with her for this book, she shared that these thoughts increased her self-awareness and allowed her a deeper connection and understanding of herself. With chaos and danger physically around her, she had complete control of her brain and the thoughts, memories, and areas of choice that came with that control.

In addition to self-awareness, she also gained a heightened sense of her situational awareness. Because of the limited dynamics of her captivity, she could stare at the sky for hours or identify patterns in nature and the environment around her. Appreciating the beautiful African sunrises and sunsets each day along with the elegance of two stars appearing in the sky at the same time each night provided her with a deeper appreciation of being aware of her environment.

For us, hopefully, the chances of being taken hostage may be close to zero. But we can all take incredible lessons from Jessica's story. Often, a near-death experience provides people with an opportunity to finally say, "What the hell. I might die, so why don't I face my fears and do some deep work on myself?" From personal experience, I have witnessed people who survive near-death experiences often declare that they'd made peace with some parts of their life and recognized that other parts were a waste. Many choose to be hyperintentional with their time and relationships in their second chance at life, no longer sweating the small stuff and being grateful for what they may have once taken for granted. What if you did not wait for a near-death experience to work on increasing your self-awareness? What if you could begin living a hyperintentional life today? Jessica would say *you have the choice*.

Jessica's Takeaways

1. Awareness Is Control

Jessica knows the chances of her ever revisiting her memories with the level of depth and detail she had in captivity are slim, but she also knows that so much good came from gaining that awareness of self. She gained a deep appreciation for who she was, how her experiences had defined her life up until that point, and what she wanted if she was to survive, and that provided clarity through her awareness. When she was rescued and reintegrated into society, she essentially felt like she was starting an entirely new chapter of her life—one filled with hyperintention and gratitude.

2. Situational Awareness Can Save Your Life

Years after being rescued, Jessica had lunch with a former intelligence officer who was teaching a course on relationship-building at Georgetown University. To Jessica's surprise, the intelligence officer said that they had some audio from her time in captivity, and multiple times they were convinced Jessica was about to be executed if not for her ability to build rapport with her captors. Jessica shared some specific examples with me that centered on her assessing the right times, when her captors were in a promising mood, to engage with them to try and build human connection or ask for more food and water. In other words, Jessica's situational awareness allowed her to build enough rapport with her captors that they decided not to kill her even when they were growing impatient with negotiations.

Hopefully you are never in similar circumstances and facing death, but what about the death of a business, death of a marriage (divorce), or the death of your reputation through poor performance, mistakes, or inappropriate behavior? Your situational awareness—or lack of it—can be a critical factor in assessing the right time to have presence, focus, make a big ask, or decide on a course of action that will have significant impact on your life.

3. Optimist or Pessimist?

Controlling what you can control means focusing on your habits, attitude, emotions, responses, actions, and thoughts. In captivity, it could have been easy for Jessica to just give up when things got hard. But she made the decisions to maintain her optimism instead of dwelling on the negatives and being a pessimist. She consciously had the awareness to assess her situation and decide how she was going to respond. Through self-, situational, sensory, and social awareness, she survived and then thrived. How can awareness better assist you in choosing optimism?

Awareness Takeaway

Awareness is a whole-life enhancer that can assist you in living with intention in every area of your life.

FORGING TWO CULTURES TO CULTIVATE PERFORMANCE
Iván López, Global President of Financial and Assistance Services at Assurant

*B*efore joining Assurant insurance and eventually becoming the president of global assistance services, Iván began his career in auditing. Iván was born and raised in Puerto Rico, allowing him to leverage his expertise on the island and his bilingualism in business. And so, when one of the largest Spanish financial institutions headquartered in Spain hired Iván to get the Spanish bank and their newly acquired Puerto Rico location working together efficiently, Iván was ready for the challenge.

The Spanish bank operated on their own systems, procedures, and processes, so trying to integrate with the newly acquired Puerto Rican bank was difficult. Iván had earlier experience in auditing and problem-solving in the back offices of KPMG, one of the Big Four accounting organizations, where he realized Spain was operating a Spanish accounting system and Puerto Rico was operating an American one. In addition, processes and procedures were not streamlined, efficient, or a prioritized area of focus, mostly because the teams were not aware of what was possible. Iván brought together representatives from both teams and laid out expectations of what he wanted the teams to accomplish, clearly articulated the plan of execution, and made both teams believe it could be done. Iván influenced corporate awareness to cultivate his team's performance and efficiency levels. He shares how all kinds of awareness, especially cultural awareness, played into the successful integration of the two teams.

Iván's Takeaways

1. **Cultural Awareness**

   Iván believes the Spanish bank underestimated the ease of integrating the Puerto Rican bank into their organization. While the two Spanish-speaking locations shared some similar customs and traditions, they were also drastically different. The Spanish bank thought entering the United States market through Puerto Rico was a good strategy, but it turned out to be as challenging as entering the US market directly. One of the first things Iván did when he began working with each bank was assist them in gaining awareness of the other's culture, customs, and habits, thereby improving situational and cultural awareness to work better with one another.

2. **Generational Awareness**

   Iván gave this insight on a form of awareness that is becoming more important each year: "Baby Boomers believe the formula to success is hard work and paying your dues with a progression through the organizational hierarchy," Iván said. "While that may have been the system for Boomers, it certainly isn't received well by millennials and Generation Z. For example, with the tech sector continuing to grow and millennials and Generation Z'ers being the most competent with technology at this time, many of them are the most competently qualified people to lead tech organizations. So, where traditional business progressions used to be through gradual progression through an organization, nowadays it is more common (or more well-known) for people of all generations to start a company, lead the company, and hire others in their generational category to join their leadership team. This plays into awareness because leaders need to maintain all the components of awareness on a consistent basis to adapt their leadership style to the team member they are engaging with, based on what generation they come from and what their specific needs are. For my fellow Boomers: Have enough awareness to recognize that 'leading' isn't like it used to be, and your style needs to change in order for you to be successful."

3. **The Higher You Go, the Less You Know**

In Iván's observations of over thirty years consulting in client-facing roles, he believes that often, the higher an individual gets within an organization and their leadership role, the less aware they are of their team members' daily roles, responsibilities, and concerns. Iván focused on communication as an example: The more competent a leader becomes in the macro dynamics of their business, the less competent they are in the micro dynamics of their business (mostly because it's no longer an area of their focus). So, when they communicate with staff outside the leadership team, a lot of what is said can be lost on the receiver; and a leader sacrifices their gravitas when they're perceived as disconnected.

Leaders who want to maintain their self-awareness seek authentic feedback from team members after communicating with them, ensuring their intent was understood by saying something like, "Can you share with me what you took away from my message?" This allows the leader to hear from the source that the message was received as the leader wanted it to be received.

Awareness Takeaway

When operating, engaging, or interacting with others in a different culture, generation, and perhaps with different cultural norms than your own, try and have an elevated sense of your situational and social awareness so you can identify cultural considerations.

THE SOMETIMES SERIOUSNESS OF MUSIC
Simon Katz, Vice President of Artists and Repertoire
at a Top Record Label Company

Simon had just landed at LAX airport in Los Angeles, California, returning from negotiations with Spotify, headquartered in Stockholm, Sweden. After the long flight, Simon turned on his phone and was instantly flooded with messages. Something was wrong. One of Simon's up-and-coming artists, who had recently released a number one hit, had publicly posted a suicide note to his social media account, and no one could reach him. This artist had threatened suicide before but had never written a suicide note. Because of past incidents, some close to him weren't taking it seriously. Simon quickly went through a mental scale he often used when decision-making: *What is the best-case scenario? And worst-case scenario?* After a few seconds of evaluation, Simon identified that worst-case scenario would be if the artist was serious this time and attempted to take his own life. Not willing to live with that on his conscience and knowing the right thing to do as a human being, Simon called the artist's father, close friends, and his team at the record label company. Within minutes, the team got the New York City police and paramedics to his door. After repeatedly knocking with no response, the police decided to bust open the door. The artist was in his bathtub, drowning after overdosing. The paramedics jumped in and saved the artist's life. Simon was later told that if the paramedics and police had arrived thirty seconds later, the artist would have died. Simon and a few from his team saved his life.

Before Simon Katz worked at this record label company, he was a multiplatinum artist, songwriter, and producer. He toured the globe and lived the artist lifestyle for close to eight years, and he had two record deals and three publishing deals. As glamorous as it may sound, touring was draining, and Simon decided to take a break. Early into his break, one of the world's leading record label companies identified that Simon had an

SIMON KATZ YOUNGBLOOD HAWKE

intellectual understanding of the music industry, not just as an artist but with a grasp of the business of music as well. The record label company hired him as an artists and repertoire executive (A&R), and within a few years, Simon became the vice president of A&R for the record label company; which at the time, was the number one record label in the world. Simon's primary duties as the VP of A&R were to find artists, develop them, sign them, and assist them in making their records. Essentially, he was responsible for their career progression. Simon was the guy who dealt with artists one-on-one.

Simon was one of the only executives in the music industry who had successfully transitioned from being an artist to recruiting artists. He found this was a competitive advantage over other record labels; most had only business professionals running their labels. Simon rarely lost a deal in closing an artist he had recruited during his six years at the record label company. The awareness and perspective Simon had gained as an artist allowed him to better understand the motivations, aspirations, and feelings of artists he was seeking to sign. When most people think *business*, they think of a transaction. Signing an artist was never just a transaction to Simon because he realized it was so much more for these artists—it was their life's work.

That day in LAX, after Simon heard his artist was going to be okay, he was flooded with emotions. He was so grateful that he and his team had made the decision to take this seriously, of course, but he also realized that the music industry faced very scary realities with many of their artists. Many incredible artists had endured trauma, were prone to unreasonable emotional intelligence fluctuations, were extremists, or had emotional and mental challenges. At that moment in LAX, Simon realized he didn't want to be in this part of the music business anymore. He completed the eight months remaining on his contract and parted ways with the record label company.

Since then, Simon has attended the Program for Leadership Development at Harvard Business School and launched his company, Grand Central Partners. He serves as a managing partner of Grand Central Partners, a private equity firm that acquires music catalogs where everyone—the artists, stakeholders, investor, and his team—wins. Simon attributes a lot of his personal success to understanding, growing, and continuously improving his GAP. At the end of our interview, Simon told me, "I didn't get into the music industry to suffer; I got into it because I love music."

Simon's Takeaways

1. Find Out Who People Are

How was Simon successful at recruiting and negotiating with some of the most creative people on earth? He first got to know them as human beings, and through that awareness, he often had the opportunity to hear about their passions, motivations, and priorities. Artists often wanted to know that whoever they were working with would take their music seriously, take them seriously, be responsible in doing what was right with their life's work, and be trustworthy. Now, ask yourself: What's really different in your line of work as it pertains to negotiating with clients or prospective partners?

While finding out who people are, sharing who you are can potentially assist in building trust and rapport through human similarities. In Simon's case, having been an artist in similar situations and with similar thoughts, Simon used the awareness gained through his own experience to meet each artist where they were at the specific time in their career progression. Taking the time to build connection can also assist in building gravitas, as it influences the perception others have of you. "I took everything on the business side personally on behalf of my artists because I am and was one of them," Simon said. "I think they appreciated that and also knew I was always going to shoot straight whether they liked it or not…that built a lot of trust and helped me with my reputation among artists in the industry."

2. The Best in the World Operate in Extremes

In sports, business, and especially in the creative world of musical artists, the best in each industry often operate in extremes. Regardless of whether we want to debate if that's right or wrong, it almost always is the case. Search for the very best performer in a specific category of anything, and chances are they work insane hours, have sacrificed social elements and relationships, and are close to obsessive with their craft. It proves to be a winning formula for them in their success as defined by society's response to their work. Simon often took this into account when he met with an artist to explore whether he wanted to move forward with attempting to sign them. He'd ask himself, *What were they saying in our first meetings, and how would they describe their vision for themselves?*

"One of the first things I would ask artists is, 'Where do you want to be in five years in the music industry?'" Simon said. "Some artists would say to go on tour or make enough income to play as a professional artist for the rest of their life. That is not what I was looking for, because the best artist in the world would respond with extraordinary vision: 'I want to be one of the greatest artists in the world' or 'I want to break industry records with the amount of success I have.'" Those types of statements were indicators that the artists were operating, thinking, dreaming, and living in extremes, and Simon saw higher probability for their success than the artists who settled for mediocre accomplishments in the industry. He said, "If artists aim for the stars and they land in the sky, they're still going to be great, but a growth mindset allowed them to get to the sky. People might think this approach is harsh, but think about it—if the artist didn't say they wanted to be the best artist in the world, they didn't have a motivation to ever get there in the first place."

Like it or not, this is often a reality with the most successful individuals, and it's important to recognize as an individual GAP practitioner embarking on a journey to greatness. Know what many who are the most successful in your line of work have sacrificed to become as successful as they are. This enhances your awareness of what success often requires. In return, it can create greater self-awareness as you identify what you are willing to do to achieve greatness and what you are not.

3. No One Cares What You Did—What Are You Doing Now?

Self-awareness often breeds humility. It's how people recognize their shortcomings. While your track record matters in business and relationships, Simon reminds us that people you interact with today want to know who you are right now and what you plan to do, not just what you did in the past. Therefore, complacency after success can tarnish one's gravitas and reputation. Simon's point reminded me of the quote, "Success breeds complacency. Complacency breeds failure. Only the paranoid survive." [45]

4. What Can I Learn from This?

One of Simon's guiding mindsets is to go into every situation and interaction with others asking, "What can I learn from this situation or this person?" He was raised by parents who rarely provided Simon with answers but challenged him to find them himself. This normalized his curiosity, and he searched for answers rather than being satisfied with not knowing. In business, he has applied this same mindset. He goes into a meeting believing the other person and what they say unless he discovers dishonesty. Entering interactions with this mindset has allowed Simon to enhance his situational awareness by better understanding people and their motivations, personality, and gravitas. "People will tell you who they are and what motivates them; you just have to give them the platform to speak and be a great listener," Simon said. "This is an easy way to gain awareness of others."

Awareness Takeaway

The seriousness of music has a lot to do with the seriousness of human interaction for Simon, who shows us how honest presence, awareness, humility, and curiosity lead us to understanding and better performance all around.

CHAPTER 4

PRESENCE

Your state of being—in mental, emotional, social, and charismatic forms.

"AND JUST LIKE THAT, I WAS NO LONGER CEO"
Justin Delaney, Serial Entrepreneur of Well-Known Companies

*H*aving just returned home to Dallas, Texas, from a business trip in New York City, Justin walked into a board meeting with his team at a company we'll call "Makam." In a matter of minutes, the private equity majority stakeholder of the board informed him that they no longer wanted him to be CEO. In the year and a half Justin had been CEO, he had led the company from a handful of locations and little revenue to hundreds of locations and a drastically increased amount in revenue. And just as things were looking to accelerate to the next level, they tell him he's no longer CEO?

You want to hear about bad timing? Thirteen years earlier, Justin finished college with a finance degree in December of 2008 at the peak of the financial crisis. And with that lemon, he made lemonade. Justin decided to take a short sabbatical and let the job market return before starting his career in business. He and his then-girlfriend (now wife) began traveling the world. To calm his girlfriend's parents, who were uneasy about their worldly explorations, Justin began writing a blog so they could follow their journey. Unintentionally, the blog exploded, and in weeks it had millions of subscribers. AOL reached out and Justin inked a deal to become one of their travel features writers. Through these travels, Justin had time to think about who he was, who and what he wanted to be, and what was important to him, increasing his self-awareness. Possibly the biggest epiphany he had was realizing how large the world was, how much he could learn from it, and how rich it was in opportunity and in creativity. It sparked his entrepreneurial spirit.

Upon returning home and after a short tenure with Delta Airlines, Justin attended business school and founded Menguin online tuxedo rental—a first-of-its-kind business primarily servicing men. Mark Cuban was one of their earliest investors. Menguin exploded, and within three years, Justin and his team sold the company to George Zimmer of Men's Wearhouse for $25 million. After exiting from his first entrepreneurial endeavor and motivated by his confidence and opportunities, Justin and his partners purchased "Makam" from its founder in 2019 and formulated a plan to exponentially accelerate the growth of the company. Justin took on the role of CEO and prioritized building a team that could withstand growth for years to come while simultaneously leading the other functions of the business.

During the height of the COVID pandemic in April 2021, Justin took a business trip to New York City. While there, he decided to visit a decades-old, privately held military surplus store to support their business, since most businesses (especially in NYC) were struggling financially from forced government lockdowns. While Justin was exploring all the items and artifacts in the store, he came across a case filled with military medals and memorabilia. To his astonishment, there was a single military name plate among the memorabilia. This name plate had his last name, Delaney, etched into it. Pleased with such a unique find, he purchased the name plate and headed to the airport to go back to Dallas, Texas. Reflecting on this moment during our interview, Justin shared that he now realizes the universe was signaling him to prepare for battle.

Justin's return to "Makam" left him in pure shock. He exited the boardroom in disbelief over the private equity group's decision to remove him as CEO. He knew the reasons they gave and didn't agree, but he couldn't help but feel defeated that he had assembled such a great team but would not have the opportunity to lead them to the bright future he had planned. He was faced with two decisions: (1) fight the private equity firm for what he believed was rightfully his and remain CEO or (2) secede. Justin chose the second, and with it came hard-learned lessons he shared with me.

Justin's Takeaways

1. Unbalanced Ownership

In my interview with Justin, I could sense his elevated heart rate and discomfort in sharing this story. Equally, I could see that this story was important for him to share because of the self-realizations and lessons he had drawn from it.

After reflecting, Justin said that if he'd had more self-awareness and presence at the time of his removal as CEO, he believes he would have fought harder for what was right instead of accepting it. For his entire life, Justin has been someone who takes full ownership of failures as his responsibility, especially when he was on or leading a team. Failure was his, and success belonged to the team. In the moment, Justin received the news of being removed as CEO as a personal failure and reverted to his muscle memory of taking ownership of the failure. He now believes he should have fought to remain CEO. Regardless of contractual agreements, Justin had made a commitment to the team members he recruited. He also thought about the implications it would have on his ability to provide for his family.

A lesson Justin learned through this experience: Spend more time understanding yourself objectively and try to analyze and increase your situational awareness so you can make unemotional or unbiased decisions, remaining present in critical moments.

2. Awareness Is Enlightenment

One of the simplest yet most complicated things Justin shared with me was, "If you do not stand up for things you believe in, what's the point in belief?" Having the awareness to identify your values and what things are important to you brings clarity. It helps you stand up for whatever you believe in. Since Justin's departure from "Makam," he has invested in more than fourteen different companies and helped many of them become ultra-successful, including Louisville Vegan Jerky, HELM Boots, and Cartainers.

Despite a challenging experience with previous partners, he continues to value investing and starting ventures with partners, rarely doing so as an individual. Collaboration is his favorite part of business, and he wouldn't have it any other way. But maintaining his self-, situational, sensory, and social awareness is always a priority to mitigate risk in partnering with those whose spiritual and/or social agendas do not align with his.

3. Presence Enables Prioritization

For somebody who is constantly thinking, creating, investing, and partnering, Justin's sense of presence is not just a want but a must. By being intentional with his presence, Justin has been successful in prioritizing three important areas of his life that are most important to him: relationships, education, and travel. Through his presence in the moment, Justin is mindful about how he is fulfilling these categories and ensuring they prioritize quality, not just quantity. He gives this advice.

- *Relationships*: Be a relentless opportunist and ask, "How can we collaborate so we can both win and benefit from each other's unique experiences?" You must invest in your relationships to achieve a return.
- *Education*: What are you doing today and what do you plan for tomorrow that will grow, develop, and increase your knowledge? What perspectives can you receive from others with an open and curious mind that will help you appreciate how people understand value, approach problems, or navigate life?
- *Travel*: Spin a globe and you'll find a different place every time your finger lands; travel will open a gateway of discovery, appreciation, creativity, and humility. Travel enables so much learning and should be engaged in as much as possible. Justin said, "I recently met someone I was considering going into business with. I didn't have a lot of time, and I knew in normal circumstances, it would take meeting with him regularly over a six-month period to analyze whether we were a good fit for each other or not. Recognizing we didn't have six months, I picked up the phone and gave him a call...I proposed we go to Japan for eight days. He agreed and off we went. You can learn everything you need to know about someone when you enter an equally uncomfortable environment with them for a sustained period of time. Though an unorthodox method, it worked, and we've been in business since." This kind of intense presence is a game changer.

Presence Takeaway

Presence enables you to prioritize your time. Create a daily routine where your day is prioritized to the maximum with things that provide value to you personally and professionally instead of wasting any of it.

BE BOLD—FOR YOURSELF AND YOUR TEAM
Samantha Weeks, Chief Transformation Officer at Shift4
and USAF's First Female Solo Thunderbird Pilot

*I*n 1981, when she was a little girl, Samantha had the opportunity to fly on a KC-135 military aircraft with her father. She
told him, "When I grow up, I want to be a fighter pilot." He
responded with, "Girls don't do that." He told her that women
were not allowed to be military fighter pilots. Not letting this information dash her dreams, Samantha set her sights on first going

to the USAF Academy, which she did in 1993—the same year females were first allowed to become fighter pilots. Samantha then secured orders for pilot training, and finishing second in the fighter/bomber training track afforded her the opportunity to become the seventh female F-15C fighter pilot ever. After that, she became the first female fighter pilot assigned to one of the oldest and most notable fighter squadrons in the US Air Force, the 94th Fighter Squadron, or as fighter pilots refer to it, the "Hat in the Ring" gang. After close to eight years flying fighters, Samantha applied for the US Air Force Thunderbird Team—the air demonstration team representing this branch of the military and world-famous for their highly skilled and technical maneuvers in the sky—and was selected to be their first female solo pilot. For the next two years, she was a trailblazer for many female fighter pilots to come.

Being a trailblazer for female leaders and pilots within the air force was not something Samantha intentionally set out to do; she just wanted to push herself and see what she was capable of. Through continued momentum and challenges, Samantha held various leadership positions in her career, ultimately leading to her most senior leadership position as the wing commander of a US base responsible for producing approximately 350 pilots each year. As the "CEO" of the base, Samantha was responsible for more than 3,000 people, 250 aircraft, $2 billion in assets, and an annual operating budget of $150 million.

As wing commander, she was told that one of the trainees in the final stages of training within her elite pilot training program no longer wanted to be a pilot. Samantha responded with, "Send him to my office. I'd like to meet with him." Peter, the student, had a rush of emotions, thoughts, and anxiety swirling within as he attempted to regain his composure before heading to Samantha's office.

She had been in her leadership position for a little over a year and had noticed it was not entirely uncommon for a pilot-in-training to decide the program was not for them. Often, though, this decision occurred in the early stages of the yearlong training. So, when Samantha was told Peter wanted to drop out of pilot training close to graduation, she was skeptical. Once a trainee fully completed the training and became a pilot, they had ten years of mandatory service ahead of them. Did Peter take advantage of the training but just not want to put in the ten years of service that came with it? Did he not have what it took to follow through with his commitment? Peter had been in the program since the beginning, and his spot could have gone to another service member with the motivation to finish the training. Before Peter was scheduled to speak with Samantha, she began speaking to her administrative staff to explore what options she had to make sure Peter was not just wasting a spot that could have gone to another trainee. Throughout those discussions, Samantha even inquired if it was an option for Peter to serve the ten-year commitment even though he technically had not completed pilot training. It was important to Samantha to be a great leader and to respond appropriately to a person she believed might be taking advantage of the processes and procedures. After creating a short list of options for Peter, she was ready to connect with him in person.

Peter entered Samantha's office in his dress uniform, clean cut, clean shaven, and noticeably nervous. Samantha knew Peter would be nervous and intimidated to meet with the highest-ranking person on the base, so she directed him to sit on the couch or in a comfy chair instead of at her large and imposing desk. "Have a seat," she said before asking, "Why do you want to quit pilot training so close to graduation?" As Peter began to stutter his reasoning, Samantha sensed his anxiety and tried to lessen the tension by relaxing her posture. Peter explained his parents had immigrated to the US from South Korea and they were nearing foreclosure on their home with no choice besides filing for bankruptcy. Though Peter was "only" the second-born son (cultural significance), he felt an obligation to financially support his parents. Samantha realized she had prepared for the wrong type of discussion. Sensing Samantha's receptiveness and curiosity, Peter leaned back in his chair and relaxed while answering her information-seeking questions.

"Do you want to be a pilot?"

"Yes," Peter replied.

"Do you want to serve your country?" she persisted.

"Yes," he said again.

"Does it have to be by flying the F-15C?" she asked, a solution forming in her mind.

"No," Peter answered.

After the meeting, Samantha got back on the phone with the admin staff to identify creative options that would serve Peter, his family, and the air force. Through a long, bureaucratic, and pains-taking process, Samantha secured a spot for Peter as a pilot in the US Air Force Reserve flying the KC-135 stationed at a base near his parents. Though it wasn't easy, Samantha believed her job as a leader was to serve others and that there was almost always a way to balance serving the individual and the institution. Her presence in the situation helped her pivot and find the flexibility to do both.

Samantha's Takeaways

1. Engaged Listening Matters

Reflecting on this exchange, Samantha shared that if she hadn't been fully present in her meeting with Peter, she would not have picked up on his nervousness and hesitations to tell his story and be completely transparent. Possessing situational and social awareness, Samantha recognized the power dynamic imbalance that may have resulted had she started the meeting behind her desk. Leaving her desk to sit next to Peter and listening to him more closely enabled Samantha to read his body language. She asked thoughtful questions that led to a better understanding of how she might help Peter. With such a busy life, it can be hard to block out the thoughts and to-do items in your head, but being fully present can increase your awareness and empower more effective leading and listening.

2. **Be Prepared, but Also Be Ready to Be Wrong**

Leaders usually have a set of beliefs, thoughts, and hypotheses going into a meeting that are often created by past experiences and trying to better understand why certain decisions were made or actions taken. Thinking through potential hypotheticals before a meeting can better prepare us for what may happen. But sometimes (maybe most of the time) we are missing data or our preparation didn't anticipate pieces of information that we discover in the moment. Samantha met with Peter prepared for possible options based on her hypothesis of Peter's motive to leave pilot training: not wanting the ten-year obligation of service. But her long tenure leading others had prepared her for the possibility that she was wrong, and based on her awareness, she needed to be present enough to adapt and pivot in real time. When Samantha reflected on this event, she said that she could have sought better information from her junior leaders to increase her situational awareness. All they shared with her was, "Peter no longer wants to finish pilot training." They did not have any context or other information to share with her. As they say in the military, no plan survives first contact with the enemy.

3. **Be Aware of the Power Your Leadership Position Holds**

Conflicting loyalties can sometimes present themselves when a leader is responsible for not only the success of their department or organization but also of their individual team members. But Samantha showed that even when it seems challenging, both can win when a leader maintains intentionality and thoughtfulness through consistent awareness and presence. Both Peter and the USAF got to win.

Presence Takeaway

Having emotionally regulated presence can assist you in having better awareness and ultimately better gravitas. It can also assist you from challenging your internal dialogue, preconceived thoughts, and imagination with the reality of what is happening in the *now*.

COMPROMISES SABOTAGE YOUR POTENTIAL
Joe De Sena, Founder and CEO of Spartan Race

Joe De Sena grew up in Queens, New York, and had what many would describe as an uncomfortable childhood. Still, he grew a multimillion-dollar pool and construction business in college and created a Wall Street trading firm before deciding to rip more than one hundred million people off their couches. Joe created Spartan, a brand that executes races like Spartan Trifectas, Spartan Trail, DEKA, Tough Mudder, and many others throughout the world. Since 2007, Joe and his team have grown to see over one million participants join their more than three hundred events each year, which are executed in over forty-five countries. Joe has completed more than fifty ultra race events himself.

From the beginning of our interview, Joe was clear that he falls within the "Aware, don't care" category of awareness. Joe is aware that some wouldn't view him as a great leader because he doesn't have the patience to motivate the unmotivated. Still, he leads a team of five hundred employees and runs an organization that operates dynamic races throughout the world. During our discussion, he shared a handful of perspectives that specifically highlighted gravitas, awareness, and presence working together.

Joe's Takeaways

1. Work Ethic Influences Gravitas

Joe grew up in Queens, New York, in a neighborhood filled with people involved in the Italian Mafia. Joe started a pool business through a weird turn of events that began with cleaning the pools of said Mafia members. Being close to that community but not involved in it enabled him to see Mafia leaders' gravitas—their self-confidence, ability to lead, and awareness of the micro details of their "organization" and the human capital within it.

Some of Joe's first employees were Polish immigrants, and he saw how much harder they worked than an average born-and-raised American. Not only did they work extremely hard, Joe said, but they were also grateful to have a job making money and to live in America, potentially because of the hardship they had experienced throughout their lives until then. Joe became aware and grateful that life is pretty good when you don't have to worry about the hardships so many others face daily. Years later, Joe still refers to "immigrant workers" as some of the hardest-working people in America as he works alongside them. They display the kind of presence and gravitas he admires—built through consistency in work ethic and exemplifying hardworking, dependable, grateful, and positive people regardless of the situation.

2. Presence Enables Gravitas

Joe's success in business and fitness has connected him with some incredible leaders: military generals, politicians, and top business professionals. "Every time I am in these environments and I witness these leaders engage with people," Joe said, "the greatest ones have a gravitas that makes every single individual in the room feel special. The individuals almost feel as if the leader's attention is solely on them and nothing else in the world exists." How do these leaders do this? They have complete and entire presence in the exact moment they are "on." How do they achieve complete and entire presence? Intentionality.

3. Aware, Don't Care: Are You in Prison? Are You Alive?

Growing up in a dysfunctional home, in a neighborhood with other parents who would literally fistfight each other, exposed Joe to some harsh realities of human dynamics. Through those experiences, Joe would compartmentalize the trauma he was exposed to and began to develop a unique ability to stop thinking about what he just witnessed or experienced and immediately move on—to not be stuck in the past but stay in the present. Joe said, "If I didn't compartmentalize the way I had growing up, those eleven years would have been a much different experience." For the last couple of decades, Joe has continued to use his *aware, don't care* approach on obstacles, negative circumstances, and uncomfortable things he experiences.

Treating his mental, physical, and emotional ecosystem the same way has enabled him to continuously look at circumstances through a simple yet realistic lens. *Am I alive today? Yes, I am...so I shouldn't complain about anything else. Am I in prison today? No, I am not...then life isn't so bad.* He is present where he is. Joe shared these mindset application methods with me after mentioning that five people from his old neighborhood served more than twenty-five years each in federal prison. "Life isn't so bad when you can have enough awareness to take a realistic perspective on a regular basis," he said. Most who do not know Joe could easily say, "Yeah, obviously, it's not prison or death, so anything is better if you look at it that way." Well, my friend, you're exactly correct, and anyone who knows Joe knows this is how he thinks and operates every single day. And it seems to be working for him.

4. **Ten Thousand Hours of Self-Awareness Work**

Tens of thousands of hours of hard physical exercise has allowed Joe to spend all that time in his head. By doing hard things, he makes himself aware that he is capable of achieving hard things during hard times in hard environments. Additionally, much of Joe's physical activity is not done with peers or while listening to music or podcasts through headphones. It's done in silence with his own thoughts, reflections, and idea creations. Through these tens of thousands of hours, Joe has been able to ask himself tough questions about his journey lived so far, revisit past experiences to seek understanding through analysis, and become more self-aware.

Presence Takeaway

Presence does not enable living in the past. Being an active practitioner of presence means you are maintaining a conscious and present state of being mentally, emotionally, socially, and charismatically. This cannot happen if you are thinking about the past. And though reflection increases self-awareness, it can decrease presence if you are reflecting while trying to engage in the present moment. Reserve time for each practice separately, not simultaneously.

*During the very last minutes of our interview together, Joe brought up Memorial Day (a federal holiday in the United States honoring service members who lost their lives while defending the United States). The holiday was a few days away, and he asked if I would do the Murph Challenge workout with him and some underprivileged kids in our local community in Orlando, Florida. When the CEO of Spartan asks you to participate in a workout named after a former teammate from the SEAL teams…you say yes. We had a blast and embodied the Spartan spirit.

GOING GLOBAL WITH A PERFORMANCE MANAGEMENT SYSTEM
Gabrielle Ivey, VP of Learning and Organizational Development at Cracker Barrel

*C*onfident in her plan, Gabrielle and her team at Lexmark had just started to implement a new performance management system for the printer and imaging company. After working on the plan for months, engaging with different internal teams throughout the world, and researching the most innovative performance management systems (PMS) in existence, Gabrielle was caught off guard when she met some resistance. After she'd shared her intent with Lexmark leaders throughout the world, why were they so resistant?

Before going to Lexmark, and before becoming a VP at Cracker Barrell, where she is today, Gabrielle began her professional career in the United States Air Force, where she enlisted and spent a handful of years working in and training others in computer operations. After transitioning out of the military, Gabrielle worked for several global organizations where she successfully delivered and engaged in technical trainings. When she was appointed director of employee development at Lexmark, a Kentucky-based global company that manufactures laser printing and imaging, she was confident her global experience in the military and commercial sector had prepared her for the task she was asked to do: implement a new performance management system (PMS) to assist with quantifying and measuring performance efficiencies and inefficiencies. Gabrielle and her team hired a top consultancy firm to research the best-designed PMS, traveled to each of Lexmark's global locations to share what was to come, and worked diligently on identifying the right system for their company. After not meeting any resistance during their engagements with the company's internal global teams, they decided to implement a system similar to what General Electric was using at the time, consisting of a team member ranking system resulting in the termination of the bottom 20 percent of performers.

Gabrielle's team started to methodically implement this PMS, but everything started to go wrong. Team members were unaware of the details and were resistant to this new PMS system that was unlike anything they had experienced before, and some felt it could affect Lexmark's long-term ability to retain talent. Despite immediate problems and heavy resistance, Gabrielle and her team maintained their commitment and persisted; this was in the best interest of the company. Eventually they were able to fully integrate the PMS and strengthen the company's organizational efficiency. Reflecting on the resistance, Gabrielle realized that her team exclusively comprised team members based at American headquarters. They fell short in understanding what team members outside of the

US had expected or wanted. Many international teams believed they had top-performing team members and felt threatened that they had to reveal their bottom 20 percent of performers, who would go under review for termination.

Gabrielle drew many takeaways from her experience in trying to implement a global program with many cultural considerations. But I also thought it was important to note that since this experience, Gabrielle has applied the lessons she'd learned through that global implementation quite often—most recently as vice president of learning and development at Tupperware, where she spent many years before taking on her current role of vice president of learning and organizational development at Cracker Barrel. Presence and awareness have paid off again and again.

Gabrielle's Takeaways

1. Put Yourself in Others' Positions

Despite global experience and having worked with numerous team members and organizations throughout the world prior to joining Lexmark, Gabrielle didn't take the time to establish authentic relationships with her global counterparts or be present with them. She categorized her interactions with team members as transactional when attempting to implement her PMS. A second attempt at a global implementation, during her tenure at Tupperware, afforded her the chance to develop relationships with team members before trying to ask something of them or engage in a change. Change is hard, and humans often need some time to "mourn" a change. That awareness will assist an implementor in maintaining positive gravitas. Seek to understand what your team members feel, want, need, and desire. Seeking to understand—and even more thoroughly when you intend to do something you've never done before—will give you situational and social awareness. Finally, through visualizing and figuratively placing yourself in the shoes of your receivers, you can gain better awareness of what they care about and be present to their concerns as you implement your ideas.

2. **Awareness Is Extra Important for Leading Globally**

Even when you have global work experience and exposure to other cultures, can you ever *really* have enough global awareness? Understanding the micro details of commerce in different countries and communities is unattainable for any single human being. To gain global awareness while leading or implementing an initiative within an organization, consider Gabrielle's awareness-builders:

- *Identify champions and early adopters.* Find a well-respected and tenured representative from each global location your initiative will be impacting and ask them to participate in something like an advisory council to assist with the project. Make it clear that you value their involvement so you can collectively create something that will be well received and impactful. This will enhance their motivation to do right by their country's stakeholders as well as make them advocate the implementation when the time comes.

- *Be mindful of cultural considerations.* Try to reflect, seek feedback, and gain formal and informal education on all the cultural considerations of each country involved so you can be respectful when communicating and implementing change.

- *Well-known doesn't mean accepted:* Gabrielle's PMS was similar to ones being adopted by some of the biggest names in business. She lacked awareness in not recognizing that just because the system was well-known and many were adopting it, that didn't mean many of the company's employees were accepting it without resistance. Challenge yourself to think through how whatever initiative or project you are implementing will be received based on cultures, norms, historical company values, and employee tenure.

3. **Balancing Authenticity and Conformity**

In closing out our interview, I asked Gabrielle if she could share some perspectives on her own experiences in developing GAP as a successful executive who happens to be a Black woman. Through the lens of developing her self-awareness as well as enhancing her presence over time, she shared the following:

• *Conformity gets you in the door, radicalism keeps you out.* If you are joining a team or organization, it is critically important to research and study their values, culture, and organizational beliefs and expectations so you know whether you are a good fit from the beginning. The hiring company often expects conformation to their organization's culture. You need to fit in to be productive and aligned with your team and culture without compromising your own values. Gabrielle also shared that conformity will assist you to get in the door, but radicalism will do the opposite. If you're continuously trying to "swim upstream" and challenge everything all the time, chances are people won't want to work with you and you'll miss opportunities to collaborate with teammates, possibly costing you advancement opportunities. Being both aware of and present to the realities of your environment pays dividends.

• *Want 100 percent self-authenticity? Be an entrepreneur.* For those who ask Gabrielle how to be 100 percent authentic, she says, "Be an entrepreneur. If you want to always do what you want, how you want, and when you want, then working within the system of an organization isn't for you." You see how absurd this can get, right? Someone might say, "Not wearing shoes is 'authentic' to me." Well, here's news for you: Walking

barefoot into your job on Wall Street isn't socially
aware, accepted, or appropriate, and it certainly is
not a part of industry norms. If you want to be in an
organization, you must adapt and react to the way the
environment actually is.

- *Find your tribes inside your organization.* Gabrielle has
maintained the level of authenticity she requires within
organizations by simply finding people who she clicks
with and knows have similar interests, styles, and habits
in and outside of work. This allows her to engage in
conversations and discussions that are authentic to
her, not just expectations of her organization's system.
Gabrielle mentioned she has found Black women, military veterans, and mentor-centered tribes at various
organizations that have allowed her to experience
different relationships; many of those tribe members
she calls friends today.

Presence Takeaway

Through maintaining your presence and interacting with your
company's culture, you can gain awareness to be proactive in the
outcomes you are trying to achieve instead of reactive.

THE PERFECT STORM
Chris Rubio, COO at William P. Clements Jr. University
Hospital at UT Southwestern Medical Center

*C*hris had worked in the health-care industry for more than twenty years when he was promoted to COO (chief operations officer) for the hospital system in December 2019, becoming responsible for the operations of an 875-bed hospital with 50 operating rooms and just under 11,000 employees. Four months into the job, COVID-19 struck the United States, and his hospital system received their first COVID-positive patient. Then, as if that hadn't been enough of a challenge, in 2021, Texas was hit with a four-day winter storm causing complete power loss and failure of the state's power grid. Anticipating the storm before it was supposed to hit, Chris woke up at 4:30 a.m. and looked at a message from his boss, the CEO: "Can you believe this is about to happen?"

The COVID-19 pandemic had proved to be a challenge worldwide. Health-care workers were continuously on the front lines, caring for patients, providing vaccines to the community, maintaining their own well-being, and doing so much more while trying to combat burnout. Chris and his team were at the center of this situation, regularly receiving vaccines to administer to qualifying patients. The University of Texas Southwestern Medical Center (UTSWMC) is in the top 10 percent of the largest hospital systems in the United States. During the early days of COVID, Chris competently led the operations of this massive hospital, and his team established four vaccination centers in the Dallas–Fort Worth area. A pandemic of this magnitude had not presented itself in the last century, so Chris and his team were experiencing nearly everything for the first time, forcing them to be creative, flexible, and motivated to create solutions on a rolling basis.

Then, in February 2021, Texas braced for what turned out to be one of the most severe winter storms in the state's history; millions of people were without power for up to four days, and 246 people died. But Chris knew his team had prepared to the best of their ability for whatever was to come. Unable to sleep the night before the storm was to hit, Chris woke up early to that text from his boss, and he headed to the hospital.

When the storm hit the Dallas area, everyone lost power. Through generators and power reserves, hospital systems such as Chris's were the first to have power restored and maintained. Chris couldn't help but think that his team was about to enter what he knew would quite literally be the perfect storm. Amid the chaos of the pandemic, Chris's team was faced with the complex challenges of COVID regulations, protocols, and care while simultaneously having to manage the complexities the storm brought. Texas has very few sand and salt trucks to assist with clearing the roads of snow and ice, so hospital team members found it challenging to get to work. They also had to maintain the safety of their own families and provide world-class care to their patients. Dozens of food, cleaning, security, and service providers, who worked to ensure the hospital system had what it needed to run efficiently, were compromised due to the storm. To make matters more complex, citizens crowded into the hospital to stay warm because temperatures were getting so dangerously low that the community was experiencing fatalities. Patients ready for discharge often had no way to get home or to get there safely. With complications compounding, Chris and his team decided to administer vaccines from one of their clinics to mitigate the possibility of waste if power ran out (unrefrigerated COVID vaccines lose their efficacy within forty-eight hours).

But Chris was confident in his team's capabilities and preparedness, and he felt at peace knowing that what they were all going through would lead them to greater competence and performance. Acknowledging that his team was currently in the incubator of chaos and demanding expectations, he knew he had to maintain his presence to stay calm and focused. Chris said, "When I sense that my team members have anxiety, I intentionally focus on being even calmer than I already am so my gravitas and their perception of me is that I am calm, collected, and confident—even if I have multiple items racing in my brain. I make a conscious effort to slow down the pace of the team's conversation, organize the work, and start assigning tasks, gathering information, and drafting communications. Despite where my thoughts and concerns may be, I know my team is looking to me for guidance, and the calmness of my physical state reassures them we are now in problem-solving mode and that we can do this." Chris knew that communication was one of the most important factors for his team, their patients, and community members, so he communicated critical information calmly and deliberately to maintain clarity and direction for those seeking information from the hospital.

After four long and highly complex days, Chris and his team (as well as the state of Texas) began to see some normalcy again, aside from the continuing COVID pandemic. Chris's team felt a sense of pride and accomplishment in having made it through a very challenging period of complexities together. As we wrapped our interview, Chris took a deep breath and said, "That was one of the most challenging moments of my life."

Chris's Takeaways

1. **Message Management**

   Humans like comfort. They do not enjoy uncomfortable situations, unknown environments, or chaos. Whether you're leading yourself or leading others, you need the situational and social awareness to recognize and anticipate how your team members may respond to situations that historically make them uncomfortable. This empowers you to clearly, deliberately, and frequently communicate to them so nothing is left to their imagination (which is often worse than reality). Chris ensured his communication was not just to his team members but also his clients (patients) and community members. Clear, deliberate, confident, and thoughtful communication can assist a leader in maintaining order, direction, and alignment in their team in any environment, but even more in a crisis. Presence allowed Chris to maintain perspective and focus on specific areas of importance, while situational and social awareness enabled him to proactively communicate to maintain high efficiency among his team.

2. **Engage the Experienced**

   Although Chris had been a part of UTSWMC for four years before his promotion to COO, there was still a lot he did not know, specifically regarding COO leadership in complex crisis situations. Through self-awareness, Chris analyzed where he was confident and where he needed help from more experienced subject matter experts and team members. If Chris had not been humble (often achieved through self-awareness), he may have become overwhelmed or failed in areas of leadership by not asking his team for help. Trusting experts on his team and empowering them to lead others reinforced the confidence in the hospital's culture that they would get through this together.

3. **Prioritization Loops**

   The balance of all three elements of GAP is important when a leader is in a crisis that continuously adapts and changes based on real-time impacts, variables, and updates. During the storm, Chris was consciously operating at the balance intersection of gravitas, awareness, and presence to prioritize and reprioritize all the components of the business, enabling him to make the *right* decisions. Chris emphasized that just because a leader makes a decision, it does not mean it cannot be changed or updated if necessary. The trick is to do it when the timing is right, the efficacy of the new information is satisfactory, and alignment in the new decision exists.

Presence Takeaway

In stressful, chaotic, or crisis situations, how you perform will dictate not only how your gravitas is received in the moment but also after the storm and into the future. Because Chris was intentional in having a calm, deliberate, and supportive presence throughout the perfect storm, he was able to elevate his gravitas among his colleagues. Much of what Chris did was thoughtful and required creative thinking and intentional planning prior to any execution.

CHAPTER 5

BALANCING GAP: GRAVITAS, AWARENESS, AND PRESENCE

GAP is optimized in each of the categories of gravitas, awareness, and presence when all are balanced and in use at the same time, enabling you to enter the balance intersection we talked about at the beginning of this book:

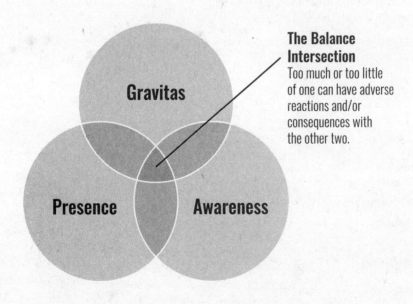

The Balance Intersection
Too much or too little of one can have adverse reactions and/or consequences with the other two.

Gravitas is the influence, emotions, and feelings someone's demeanor evokes in others.

My concept of **awareness** is composed of four types of awareness, what I like to call SA4:

- Self-Awareness: The perception of self being aligned with the perception of others
- Situational Awareness: Understanding the context and details of an event or action
- Social Awareness: Understanding of the context and details of an exchange between two or more people, often determined by the environment
- Sensory Awareness: The sensory responses (emotion, voice changes, body position, eye contact, etc.) to a situation or event

Presence is your state of being—in mental, emotional, social, and charismatic forms.

Balanced together, they can spur unstoppable growth and create magnificent opportunities.

MY THIRTY-MINUTE MEETING WITH BOB IGER
Dan Cockerell, Vice President of the Magic Kingdom, Walt Disney World, Florida

*D*an was notified by his leader that Bob Iger, the CEO of Disney, was coming for a thirty-minute tour of the Magic Kingdom, Disney's prized jewel and the theme park Dan led. The guidance Dan received was, "Get in the mindset that this meeting is just between you and Bob. Bob travels for these tours with an entourage of team members, but just maintain your focus on making it a meaningful tour with Bob." When Dan reflected on this meeting, he vividly recalled how Bob made him feel like Dan was his only priority and that there was nothing else on his mind except Dan, the Magic Kingdom, and the topic they were discussing at any given time. Dan said the balance of gravitas, awareness, and presence exemplified by Bob Iger was the kind he wanted to emulate. "We can't be what we can't see," he said.

As the vice president of Magic Kingdom, Dan was responsible for twelve thousand team members, more than twenty million visitors each year, $2 billion in annual revenue, and the largest theme park in the world, which is open every day. Starting as a parking attendant and rising through nearly every level of the organization over his twenty-six-year career at the Walt Disney Company, Dan considered his own playbook for mastering gravitas, awareness, and presence. Rather than share one specific case study example from him, I thought it best to summarize the ten GAP practitioner tips and insights Dan shared during our interview.

Dan's Takeaways

1. **Preparation Is Awareness**

   Some of the greatest executives Dan worked with in his career had discipline as a common denominator. They would often prepare for meetings with competence and knowledge. They most often rose through the levels of the organization to get to the executive level, and in doing so, had gained competence to recognize a well-done job at each level. But that aside, they still made it a priority to enter each meeting understanding what they did know, what they did not know, and what they thought important to know.

2. **GAP Practitioners Don't Focus on Others' Egos (Gravitas)**

   Confidence is often gained through competence and credibility. Credibility comes from being trustworthy, dependable, self-accountable, and delivering on what you said you would do. Those leaders who have incredible gravitas are credible in their environment, with their peers, and with themselves. Because they are confident and have a demonstrated track record to prove their dependability, they are often confident in new territory and embarking on new endeavors. Maybe not confident in the technicalities or complexities at first, but confident in their ability to overcome whatever adversity they may face to accomplish the task. Therefore, while they acknowledge or are aware of naysayers, doubters, or other egos that may be on their team, they do not allow them to block their performance. Rather, they increase their awareness of the critics' points of view to assist in their strategy of execution, but they do not allow critiques to jeopardize their emotional composure. In return, this increases their gravitas among others.

3. **Awareness Assists in Knowing Your Place in the Ecosystem**

The Hollywood depiction of a leader is someone who takes charge, has the right answers, makes all the decisions, and the list goes on. But leaders with great self-awareness know their strengths and weaknesses. Leaders with great situational and social awareness know when to enter a meeting or environment and listen rather than speak, to empower rather than micromanage, and to prompt collaboration instead of control it. Dan reflected on past leaders who would often enter a scheduled meeting and not sit at the board table but instead against the wall to symbolically show they were there to listen and learn, not to control the direction of the meeting or press their bias on the agenda. Without awareness, a leader cannot assess what is appropriate in the ecosystem they enter at a specific time.

4. **Internal Dynamics Do Not Matter to the Customer (Awareness)**

Often, leaders can become disconnected from what *really* matters. For Dan and his team at Disney, the priority was always the customer experience. Dan often found himself reminding his team at the end of scheduled meetings that while job titles, company politics, and internal team dynamics were important to address, the customer doesn't really care as long as their experience is satisfactory. If the stakeholder and customer awareness ever became a secondary thought for Disney team members, bad things could happen to the business's revenue and growth. Awareness is not just a check in a box but a continuous stream of consciousness important for individual and team performance.

5. **Appearance Influences Gravitas**

Dan chuckled during our interview when he started to speak on appearance because he knows there are a lot of opinions on what is right or wrong when it comes to physical appearance, dress, and grooming standards. Right, wrong, or indifferent, Dan was clear that it matters and, by nature, people judge appearance. Books like *Blink* by Malcolm Gladwell or *Executive Presence* by Sylvia Ann Hewlett discuss first impressions and appearance backed by data that confirm Dan was statistically correct.

Social awareness is required to gauge what appropriate appearance is required based on a specific engagement. When Dan traveled to the Imagineering headquarters where Disney creatives think and design the future of their theme parks, he dressed more informally to fit in with the culture he would be joining for the day. When at the park, he wore a uniformed short-sleeved button-down shirt and tan dress pants. When in the boardroom, he wore his suit, sometimes with a tie, sometimes without. Regardless of whether the clothes were "authentically" him was, to an extent, irrelevant because he wore what was socially acceptable, expected, and appropriate. Knowing what to wear, how to show up, and being intentional about the professionalism it exemplifies increases a person's gravitas.

6. **Stack the Cards in Your Favor: Minimize Distractions to Maximize Presence**

   Dan's smartwatch is no longer a part of his wardrobe. He acknowledged a universal signal for "I am bored" or "When will this end?" was looking at your watch in the middle of a meeting. Dan noticed that whenever his smartwatch buzzed or dinged, he almost instinctively glanced at it. This interrupted his ability to be present and also didn't do his gravitas any favors with those he was meeting with. So, Dan consciously decided to revert back to wearing analog watches that are much less distracting. This is one example Dan highlighted to point out that in a technologically driven world, there are hundreds of these micro distractions; it is up to each of us to be aware of what they are and minimize them where appropriate to maximize our presence.

7. **Think Through Situations Before They Happen (Presence)**

   Dan had pushed his desk against the wall in his office so it was impossible for anyone who entered to be on the other side of his desk. He also had a small round table with two chairs for one-on-one meetings. He never wanted the traditional power dynamic of the boss or leader sitting behind the desk with the office visitor on the other side, so he removed the physical dynamics that make that possible. And when meeting with someone one-on-one, he wanted a neutral and equal environment to collaborate in. He wanted the environment to empower his visitors to focus on what was really important—the collaboration. These two examples of Dan's intentional office layout show the significance of a leader thinking through human interactions and exchanges before they happen, increasing awareness, gravitas, and presence as a result.

8. Be Mindful of Unintended Consequences of Your Words (Awareness)

When Dan was the general manager of Disney's Fort Wilderness Resort in Orlando, Florida, he and his team were two months away from Christmas season. He had informally met with the head chef of the resort in the lobby entryway. Out of curiosity, Dan asked the head chef what the food plans were to make the Christmas season at the resort more magical for their guests. After the chef shared the planned events and food changes with Dan, Dan asked the chef about incorporating build-your-own gingerbread houses for the kids. Dan continued to think out loud and shared fond memories he had as a kid building a gingerbread house with his parents and how it could be a great feature for the resort to consider in the future for the kids staying there during the holiday season. Thinking nothing of it, Dan left his exchange with the chef and continued with his scheduled day.

The next day, Dan received a phone call from the resort's manager of food and beverage: "Hey Dan, I sure wish you would have mentioned it to me that we were going to be including a build-your-own gingerbread house exhibit for the kids this year in our lobby. The head chef has already ordered the materials and is putting the plan you discussed with him into action…this puts the team in a unique situation we had not previously planned for." Dan put his hand over his face in disbelief but also in acknowledgment of his lack of self-awareness. Of course, if the general manager of the resort indicated he thought something would be a good idea, the team member he expressed it to would act on it. After apologizing to the manager for his slip up to the manager of food and beverage, Dan promised himself to be more aware of every word he used with his team and the potential implications they could have.

9. **Attitude Breaks Barriers (Presence)**

Regardless of the industry or job, when Dan assembles his team, he looks for team members with great attitudes—positive and determined to do what is necessary to be successful. If a team member doesn't have the technical skills or abilities, a positive attitude allows them to develop the necessary skills or find someone who has them. If the team member identifies an area of development and growth for themselves, they do not need to be told to begin working on it because their attitude insists they need to be proactive to be better. People who will set out to increase their GAP more than likely have a great attitude; they are seeking knowledge to assist them in growing their GAP. Great team players with great attitudes are aware that positive attitudes are valuable to the team and negative attitudes are detrimental to the team.

10. **Awareness Increases Reputational Outcome (Gravitas)**

Self-, situational, social, and sensory awareness influence an individual's gravitas. If you have awareness components continuously engaged, chances are you will be better at understanding how people feel and more intentional with how you make people feel. Being a consistent and intentional practitioner of GAP will increase your reputation among those you interact with.

Balancing GAP Takeaway

All Dan's GAP experiences and observations prepared him for his pivotal thirty-minute meeting with Bob Iger. By leveraging the power of the GAP "special sauce," Dan was able to constantly observe GAP enhancement tips, tricks, and tools throughout his career to craft into his own and apply them to enhance his own GAP. This book will certainly serve as a foundation of knowledge as it relates to GAP, but don't forget that GAP has objectivity, innovation, and continuous considerations. Regardless of innovation and changes in work environments, if you are mindful of the balance intersection and the GAP Enhancement Cycle, you will have a competitive advantage over those who do not.

THE DAY I WALKED OUT OF THE EXECUTIVE TEAM MEETING
Anne Marie Jess Hansen, CEO of Copenhagen
Business School Executive Foundation

*A*nne Marie Jess Hansen had just walked out of the executive team meeting with assertiveness, confidence, and disappointment. Her CEO was out of line and created an environment that provided her with only two solutions: accept his behavior or lose her emotional composure (which ultimately could have resulted in losing her job). She created a third option by maintaining her composure and exiting the room: statement made and enablement of unfair behavior rejected.

Born and raised in the country of Denmark, Anne Marie's childhood encouraged her to create the life she wanted to live, to be bold and confident in her values, and, most of all, to lead.

Holding a degree in economics and a PhD in corporate strategy from Copenhagen Business School, Anne Marie began her career as a strategy consultant at Deloitte before transitioning to Danisco (later acquired by Dupont), where she worked developing technology-based strategic solutions for their clients. This opened opportunities for Anne Marie to become an executive at Forca and, eventually, ATP, two Danish pension companies. Anne Marie rose to senior vice president of customers and projects during her tenure at Forca while also teaching as an associate professor at Copenhagen Business School.

Under mounting pressure from the board of directors at Forca and of other stakeholders, the CEO had agreed to take on a project they could not afford. The Forca team estimated the project required a budget of approximately eighty million Danish kroner, but the client had allocated only forty million to make it work. With pressure to grow the business's revenue, the CEO agreed to take on the scope of the project, knowing it would be a challenge to deliver with half the budget. He took ownership of the project and maintained the primary leadership roles and responsibilities for the first six months; Anne Marie and her colleague, whom we'll call "Dorte," assisted him as secondary leaders, spearheading initiatives in their domains of expertise.

On a weekly basis, the executive team held a three-hour meeting in the boardroom to discuss project updates, business projections, and other matters relevant to the performance of the organization. When the team of five gathered for their board meeting following the first six-month period on this project, the CEO said, "Why is this special project failing to perform? Dorte, this has been your responsibility since day one, and you have not led us to an advantageous position." Dorte's face turned white and she looked down at her papers. In disbelief, Anne Marie felt the room's air become completely still and had to take a sip of water and plant her feet on the ground. The CEO began to continue with the agenda items when Anne Marie gained enough composure to raise her hand to speak.

"Thank you. Did I just hear you correctly in signaling that Dorte has been responsible for leading this special project?"

The CEO replied, "Yes, she has been the primary leader since the beginning."

Anne Marie looked at Dorte, who was still staring at her papers and then to the two other executives in the boardroom who avoided eye contact with her. Knowing herself, Anne Marie took a few seconds to reflect and analyze. *I have two options: (1) I can stay silent and "professional" while enabling this meeting to continue with Dorte as the scapegoat or (2) I can lose my emotional composure and share how I really feel about this unfairness...which could ultimately result in losing my job as retaliation.* Not satisfied with either option, Anne Maire trusted her instincts and decided to create a third option: She got up from the table, collected her belongings, and exited the room.

Anne Marie entered her office, shut the door, and tried to regain her composure and clarity of thought. Still feeling the adrenaline from what she had just experienced, she messaged two close colleagues to come to her office right away with coffee and water. As she wrapped up receiving counsel from her colleagues, her CEO's assistant called to notify Anne Marie that the CEO wanted to meet with her right away.

As Anne Marie went and met with her CEO. As she entered his office, he said, "Anne Marie, I've been working with you for quite some time now, and I have never seen you get up and leave from an important meeting without any explanation. What's going on?"

Anne Marie remained standing and replied: "You stated that Dorte was solely responsible for the special project when the truth is *you* have been responsible for it since day one."

The CEO responded vaguely and did not take ownership on what was so obvious to the entire executive team over the last six months of the project. Unsatisfied with the CEO's lack of leadership and personal accountability, Anne Marie turned and walked out.

Two years later and after sustained negative performance, the board of directors chose to replace the CEO. Anne Marie established herself within the firm as someone people wanted to follow because they knew she would always be leading from character, representing strong values, and, most importantly, she would stand up for what was right and challenge a bully if one presented themselves. She proved that her GAP was a stabilizing force in her organization. Shortly after the reorganization, Anne Marie left and now continues to lead as the CEO of Copenhagen Business School's Executive Foundation, where she regularly incorporates educational experiences, courses, research, and teachings to empower global leaders to act with values and maintain their authenticity in difficult business situations.

Anne Marie's Takeaways

1. **Fairness Is Nonnegotiable: Values over Business**
   Business transactions take place thousands of times over the course of someone's career. Values transactions are put into play in almost every exchange. You can afford a slip here and there when it comes to business transactions, but one really cannot afford to slip when it comes to values. In my experience, leaders who make values-based decisions are less likely to regret their decisions and often attract other team members who have similar values. One of Anne Marie's core values is fairness. Fairness in all things includes business engagements. Her CEO treated a colleague unfairly and she decided to act—knowing his behavior had violated her values and she could potentially be fired in retaliation. Without maintaining consistent self-awareness, a leader chances not having an up-to-date and thorough understanding of what their values are, what they believe, and how they must act to be a practitioner of

their values. Though difficult, Anne Marie's priority was to always live her values. If she did not, she would be left with regret and disappointment. Her self-awareness and strong values motivated three colleagues to follow her to her last three places of employment, saying, "Where you go, I go, because I know you have my back and I'm in good hands following your values-based leadership."

2. **Silence Is Enablement**

When reflecting on this event during our interview, Anne Marie shook her head when I pointed out to her that there were two other male executives in the room who tolerated a behavior they knew was wrong and unethical. I asked Anne Marie if she ever spoke with the two executive colleagues afterward, and she said she did. One of them was adamant that she was out of line in challenging the CEO's direction and authority, while the other shared with her that he has massive regret over this situation and that if he is ever in a situation similar to that one in the future, he hopes he will act with as much courage as Anne Marie did. Silence in the presence of wrongdoing is acceptance of the wrongdoing, ultimately enabling the individual to repeat the same actions into the future. In order to act in a challenging moment, an individual has to maintain full presence and awareness so a harmful agenda isn't just continued because of the inaction of bystanders.

3. **Positional Privilege Requires Responsibility**

Society, the organization, the team members, and the responsibilities of the position demand leaders to uphold the responsibility that comes with their position. As a senior vice president responsible for leading others and maintaining the standards her peers expect of her, it was and is important for Anne Marie to be a practitioner of the gravitas, awareness, and presence that are required for her to be able to execute her roles and responsibilities and exercise her authority. As she continues to grow throughout her journey, she leverages her lived experiences to heighten her awareness of and comfort with what others expect of her and what she expects of herself in high-stakes environments like the board room. If you are sitting at the table in a board room or executive meeting, you have an obligation to act and speak when the situation demands. After all, that is why you are there.

Balancing GAP Takeaway

The GAP Enhancement Cycle is so crucial to mastering your GAP. If Anne Marie hadn't been regularly experimenting, evaluating, and educating herself on GAP experience and outcomes, she may not have been ready to fully utilize each component of GAP in a moment that demanded it, with so much on the line. Have you ever been in a situation where you had not responded the way you would have liked and only recognized that at a later time? Of course you have! We all have. And this point emphasizes the importance of understanding the complexities of your own GAP so you are ready to act in a way you will later be proud of when the environment demands it.

GROWING UP IN THE PROJECTS
Christopher Brown, COO of North America's Talent Solutions at Aon

Christopher was born and raised in South Boston, Massachusetts, in the Old Colony housing projects as a Black-Italian kid with no father and a white mother who worked three jobs to provide. Life wasn't easy in this part of Boston, infamous for being the toughest, hardest, poorest of neighborhoods; many of its residents were involved in gangs, drugs, and crime just to put food on the table. Pair that with the Irish-based gang controlling the area, Christopher was exposed to constant racism, discrimination, and hatred just for being Black. It wasn't abnormal for Christopher's friends to lose their lives to gang-related violence even at a young age. When Christopher was eighteen years old, he had two choices: (1) stay in this environment and operate in a world he knew or (2) escape. After his childhood best friend was shot dead, the choice was simple: It was time to escape.

Old Colony projects located in "Southie" outside of Boston, Massachusetts.

Determined to escape the world he had always known, Christopher applied to multiple universities and was accepted into Northeastern, where he studied accounting. Searching for employment after college, he landed an interview with The Hartford, a commercial business insurance firm. He purchased his first-ever suit, groomed himself to the best of his ability, and walked into the interview feeling confident of how far he had come up until this point. Christopher sat down, handed the interviewer his résumé, and began answering questions that were posed to him. The interviewer took a second look at Christopher's résumé and glanced up with a curious look on his face. "Is this your real address? Like where you live?"

The address on Christopher's résumé was the Old Colony housing projects. Christopher responded, "Yes."

Clearly familiar with the "bad sides of town," the interviewer quickly brought the interview to a close and thanked Christopher for coming in. Christopher knew what this was—he'd experienced it a thousand times before. Without even knowing him, the interviewer had judged Christopher based on where he came from and perhaps the color of his skin.

Christopher turned to leave at the same time executive John Capuzzo exited a meeting. Paralleling Christopher's path to the elevator, John asked Christopher if he had just finished an interview and whether he had a résumé. Christopher handed John his résumé, who glanced at it and then said, "Is this your address? Were you raised here?"

Christopher could not help thinking, *Here we go again*, but replied politely, "Yes, sir."

John looked Christopher in the eye and said, "If you were born and raised at this address, attended Northeastern, majored in accounting, and are standing in front of me in a suit, you have defied more obstacles and adversity than most people could ever comprehend. I don't know how your interview went, but you're hired."

During Christopher's first few weeks on the job, he went in early and left late; he wanted to honor the opportunity he had been given (and earned). The Boston Hartford office had a delinquent *Fortune* 500 client who would not pay a $28,000 invoice, and by the time Christopher joined the team, the outstanding invoice had become an office joke. Team members often referred to it as "the impossible" or the "invoice that will never be paid." As a ritual, the Boston office would often assign this outstanding invoice account to newly hired team members almost as a form of friendly hazing. So, when Christopher was assigned the account, he said to John and his colleagues, "I am going to get this invoice paid." Laughing at his ignorance, John said, "If you can get it paid, I will buy you a steak dinner."

Before the day was over, Christopher examined what previous team members had done to try and collect payment and quickly realized that their form of communication had been almost entirely email. The next day, Christopher picked up the phone and called the client's office, requesting to speak to the CEO. After dozens of attempts, Christopher was finally connected to the CEO. He introduced himself, then referenced the outstanding invoice and politely requested it be paid. The *Fortune* 500 CEO snickered at Christopher's audacity and hung up. For days that followed, Christopher called his office every day until he finally left a voice message. "Hello, sir. This is Christopher Brown again. If I don't hear from you by tomorrow, I will personally come down to your office and wait in your lobby until this invoice gets paid."

Hartford team members thought Christopher was crazy because this CEO was known as somebody who was not to be trifled with and who even carried a revolver on his belt every day.

After leaving the voice message, Christopher received a phone call from the CEO: "I don't know how they train you over there at The Hartford or who you think you are, but it is so unusual for a young kid to be calling me every day for a lousy $28,000 invoice. The check is in the mail, now leave me alone!"

John and Christopher went out to enjoy the promised steak dinner. At the office the next day, Christopher felt everybody looking at him as the person who accomplished the impossible. He thought, *So this is gravitas?*

After close to ten years at The Hartford, Christopher received an opportunity to join Aon Insurance, and after ten years with them, he became their North America Talent Solutions chief operating officer.

Growing up in a neighborhood where inaccurately reading, assessing, and analyzing situations—having poor situational awareness—could cost you your life, Christopher was hyperaware of these three members' intentions. Through his social and sensory awareness of their body language, tone of voice, and behavior, he discerned their intentions. He decided to prepare for what he predicted the three could do, and he instructed his team to explore potential actions these three leaders might take. As a result, Christopher's team was well equipped to respond to the actions and accusations of the unethical leaders with facts, emotional composure, and a steady, executed strategy. Christopher's awareness saved his organization a couple million dollars and heightened his gravitas among his colleagues.

Christopher's Takeaways

1. Awareness First

Christopher believes that people first need to have awareness before they can have presence and certainly before they can have gravitas. Self-, situational, social, and sensory awareness allow you to become more in tune with any intentionality surrounding your presence. "Once the awareness and presence components of GAP are built, refined, and put into action, they almost become second nature," Christopher shared. With awareness and presence as the foundation, your gravitas can be leveraged and activated by the judgments, acts, and choices resulting from others' perceptions. But Christopher was clear in saying, "What is often misunderstood is [the idea] that awareness, presence, and gravitas are natural gifts. While some of these areas might seem natural to some, they can each be learned, improved, and applied."

Growing up, Christopher grew and developed awarenesses through instinct, survival, and navigating a very challenging environment. During our interview, he freely shared that saying the wrong thing or having the wrong kind of gravitas in a situation could have gotten him killed.

Going from the projects to a profession in the commercial sector, Christopher has lived by many of the same lessons he learned growing up: Do not be disrespectful to others, do not talk behind your colleagues' backs, do not take credit for work you did not do. The foundation of awareness from Christopher's youth has played a direct role in his ability to apply many GAP lessons and skills to his professional work environments, often enabling him to gain a competitive advantage.

2. **Repetition**

Putting knowledge and learnings into action is never easy. It requires intentionality paired with action, followed by repetition. Christopher points out that through continuous repetition, evaluation, and feedback (often critical and hard to hear) someone comes to understand and enact a willingness to change. Without willingness to engage in the uncomfortable, you won't be successful in improving your GAP.

3. **Authenticity: Person or Persona?**

With so many "how-to" resources available that offer step-by-step self-help guides, Christopher believes people can get lost in trying to be something or someone they aren't. He emphasizes the importance of taking the time and thoughtfully trying to increase their self-awareness, to thoroughly understand who they are, what they believe, and what values guide them in their day-to-day lives. Your gravitas will not be positively enhanced if you are a persona and not a person, so get clear on who you are and what you stand for. Then those who you interact with will know you are authentic.

Balancing GAP Takeaway

Often, we are not in life-or-death situations and scenarios that require the full embodiment of GAP. But what if you could internalize the same discipline required if you were in life-or-death situations to hold yourself accountable to the GAP components? Though Christopher is no longer in the projects, the lessons he had internalized for survival are now what he leverages to continue his success in the commercial sector.

THREE BAD DAYS IN THIRTY YEARS
Jon Cute, Orlando Police Department SWAT Officer

*J*on and his team were ninety minutes away from wrapping up their evening shift at 5:30 a.m. when Jon made the decision to try and draw out the drug dealer they had been casing, trying to get him to come out of his apartment so they could make a safe arrest. In the matter of moments, gunshots were exchanged, and the situation escalated, ultimately leaving Jon with a handful of awareness realizations that would change the course of his career forever.

Born and raised in East Providence, Rhode Island, Jon knew by the age of five that he wanted to become a police officer because the police were the only people his abusive father was afraid of. The gravitas of a cop always stood out to him; a cop was someone community members could depend on to take care of those in need and to be a force to be reckoned with when mischief ensued. In 1990, Jon decided to fulfill his childhood dream and joined the 110-person police department in East Providence. After serving his local community for close to seven years, he moved to central Florida to become the director of security for Rosen Hotels and Resorts. Though he learned many lessons there, he believed his calling was still in law enforcement, so he applied to join the Orlando Police Department (OPD). Within two and a half years, Jon's hard work earned him a spot on the drug unit team, requiring him to go undercover at times.

During this particular operation, before it went wrong, Jon and the OPD team he was a part of were watching an apartment complex. They'd received a tip from an informant that drugs were being sold there. The OPD team sent a confidential informant to purchase drugs, and once the sale completed and the drugs were exchanged, they had the proof of unlawful activity they needed. While Jon was sitting with some of his team members in his vehicle, distanced from the apartment complex, one of his teammates said to him, "Hey Jon, don't forget my mother is flying in from New Jersey this morning at 7:00 a.m. and I have to pick her up. We often go over because the job demands it, but can we please make sure we conclude our shift on time tonight?" In quick acknowledgment, Jon said, "Yeah, man, it won't take that long."

Once the confidential informant notified Jon and his teammates that the suspect was indeed in the apartment selling drugs, Jon proceeded to the front door of the apartment with the rest of his squad. On his way there, Jon was rehearsing what he was going to say once he and another one of his teammates got the drug dealer to open the door. Jon's plan was to get the drug dealer to come outside so they could make a clean arrest. Once to the door and after a few knocks, the drug dealer cracked open the door, suspicious of who was outside.

Jon and his teammate identified themselves and asked to come inside, but the drug dealer denied their request. After an exchange and slight escalation, Jon drew his taser and fired it at the drug dealer. As the drug dealer fell to the ground behind the door, Jon immediately made entry into the apartment. The drug dealer pulled out a firearm and began to fire over his shoulder at the doorway. Jon took cover, drawing his firearm, returning fire, and shouting "gun!" to warn his teammates. The drug dealer got up and began to run down the hallway of the apartment, Jon and his teammate in pursuit. They reached him just as he was opening the bedroom window in an attempt to jump out and escape. The drug dealer began firing his illegal firearm back at Jon and his teammate, and they returned fire, striking the drug dealer and injuring him as he fell out of the second-story window. After a quick search, OPD was able to locate the drug dealer outside the building and make the arrest.

Like many exchanges law enforcement is faced with daily, the situation escalated from zero to a hundred in seconds. As Jon drove with one of his colleagues back to OPD headquarters to go through protocols required of officers after they've had to use their weapons, Jon began to reflect on the step-by-step progression of the scenario. And then tears began to form in his eyes. His fellow officer sitting next to him in the car noticed and said, "Jon, are you okay?" Jon turned to her and said, "My selfish attitude could have gotten others killed today."

When Jon arrived at OPD's headquarters, so did his teammate who needed to pick up his mother at the airport at 7:00 a.m. It was now 7:30 a.m., and the team of officers wouldn't be allowed to leave for the next few hours because they needed to go through the department's protocols. Jon felt he had let his teammate down, in more ways than one.

This event would be the catalyst for changing Jon's attitude, mindset, and, ultimately, his career. At the time of this scenario, Jon did not have a family of his own, so he prioritized the job and performing well, and nothing else. Jon learned several lessons that morning that we will explore further in his takeaways. Using what he learned, he would soon go on to join the SWAT team, where he would reach the title of assistant squad leader. While on SWAT, Jon and his team were one of the primary tactical response teams that arrived at the infamous Pulse nightclub mass shooting. In total, Jon would serve on SWAT for eighteen years. Having achieved the rank of lieutenant, Jon is now one of the department's top fifty leaders out of just under one thousand law enforcement officers. Orlando Police Department consistently ranks as one of the top law enforcement agencies in the United States.

Jon ended our interview with tears in his eyes, expressing how much he loves being in law enforcement, primarily because it affords him the ability to serve a community he loves with people he loves, his fellow officers. After thirty years on the job, Jon said to me, "I've only had three bad days in my thirty years." Jon was referencing the day his colleague Lieutenant Debra Lucinda Clayton was killed, the day his colleague Officer Kevin Andres Valencia was killed, and the day of the Pulse nightclub mass shooting. Jon recognized that the day described in this case study was not among the truly bad ones; it was an incredible learning opportunity for him. Fortunately, none of his teammates were hurt or injured, and they got a bad guy off the streets.

Jon's Takeaways

1. Attitude Is Controllable

In the early days of Jon's career as a law enforcement officer, he was motivated to be the best he could be, even if it would mean having to place his wants of performance over team member's wants and realities. During our interview, Jon expressed that early in his career he was lacking self-awareness by not properly understanding how others viewed and perceived him based on his actions. His actions were often driven by selfish desires for performing at his job—making the arrest, achieving the goal, wrapping up the case—and he very rarely took into account other considerations his team members may have had.

Jon shared the example above because it was a pivotal moment in his career, when he recognized his get-it-done attitude was going to get someone killed, cost him his job, or at the very least contribute to a poor reputation. So, recognizing the severity of his actions after that incident, he made a conscious effort to maintain a team-first positive attitude from that day forward. He began to consistently, consciously improve his self-, situational, social, and sensory awareness, and that led inevitably to trust with his teammates and a sense of gravitas they could rely on. He worked on maintaining a positive attitude—one that makes you someone other team members want to be around. It determines the outcomes of not only your performance but also your team's.

2. **Your Actions Affect the Team's Performance**

When Jon's teammate said that he needed to pick up his mother from the airport at 7:00 a.m., Jon's presence was fully engaged in the progression of the scenario, not the conversation with his teammate. Although he heard him, Jon didn't truly listen to him—he didn't adjust his plan of action or take steps to make sure he could be a good teammate by not rushing things to make an arrest and put his teammates in a tough position. Jon's intent was to succeed at their job in a short amount of time so his teammate could get to the airport. But Jon's intent was not followed through with his actions, because he didn't account for the "what ifs" of his plan. Recognizing his inability to be a good teammate in this scenario, Jon became more situationally and socially aware of his teammates' realities from that day forward. Did they have families and timelines they needed to worry about? Were their desired outcomes the same as his in each scenario or circumstance they faced? This heightened awareness allowed Jon to be more thoughtful, mindful, and aware of aligning intentions with action as well as team member outcomes in order to increase the team's overall performance.

3. **Reputation Matters**

In most industries, and especially in law enforcement, your reputation is everything. When Jon was undercover on the street, informants needed to know they could trust him or they wouldn't share important information with him. When Jon was among his peers and fellow officers, they needed to know he was trustworthy, dependable, reliable, and a team player. Since the day of the situation above, Jon has made a conscious effort every single day to uphold an outstanding reputation and project the gravitas required to do his job well. As an Orlando Police Foundation board member, I have regularly seen Jon interact with his colleagues for more than four years and can say with full confidence that he is loved—by the community, his family, and, most of all, his fellow officers. Jon learned through hard knocks the importance of recognizing a failure, adjusting your attitude to never let it happen again, and being a great teammate. In doing so, he's increased his self-awareness and, ultimately, his gravitas among the just under one thousand other officers at OPD.

Balancing GAP Takeaway

Taking ownership of your mistakes, having the awareness to think through the potential implications, and identifying lessons has the ability to positively influence your gravitas—as long as you identify the lessons and implement them so they become lessons truly learned.

"I RAN MYSELF INTO THE GROUND"
General Robin Rand, US Air Force (Retired)

*A*fter twelve months of being a wing commander (CEO equivalent) of Kunsan Air Base in South Korea and leading three thousand military personnel, Robin returned home and had five days before reporting to Luke Air Force Base (Luke AFB), in Arizona, to become the 56th Fighter Wing commander. At the time, Luke AFB had 206 F-16 fighter jets, approximately ten thousand personnel, more than sixty thousand military retirees who lived close to the base, and fourteen municipalities that surrounded the fence line of the base. Meetings with US Senate and House of Representative staffers and members, local mayors, and city council members were regularly expected of the wing commander. At that point in Robin's career, he was nominated to begin the process to become a one-star general.

Eleven months after taking command of Luke AFB, Robin arrived home on the evening of Cinco de Mayo to more than seventy guests. Robin told his wife, Kim, "I am so exhausted. I don't feel good right now, and I don't know if I'm up for tonight's party."

Kim said, "You continue to do this. I've been telling you for over a year that you're going too hard. You are going to mingle with all our guests tonight...you can rest afterward."

Robin attended the party, then went to bed. He did not get up for four days. He had run himself into the ground, and his body was shutting down.

After close to two full years of wing command in the US Air Force, Robin's ability to continue at the pace he was going was unrealistic. Not just unrealistic—his body was telling him it was physically impossible. During his four straight days of rest, there wasn't much for Robin to do except reflect and think. He gained a deeper understanding of himself, enhancing his self-awareness and revealing that he had let so many people down. By not taking care of himself through appropriate sleep, a nourishing diet, and regular exercise, his body forcibly removed him from his duties to lead at his maximum capacity.

When Robin recovered, he went to his office and assembled his colleagues, direct reports, fellow executives, and assistants with the intention of one thing: to apologize. Robin said, "Team, I need to apologize. I failed you, and I need your help. When I don't listen to you and you try to make adjustments on my behalf to lighten my load and calendar, I need you to remind me of what just happened to me, because I can't allow it to happen again. Not only did I fail you, but I failed all of the military personnel I am leading, and I will not let that happen again." When Robin went home after work that evening, he apologized to his closest teammate, his wife.

Immediately after the Luke AFB assignment, Robin deployed in combat to Balad Air Base, Iraq, for his third consecutive wing command tour. He led for an additional thirteen years in the US Air Force, attaining the rank of four-star general and culminating as the commander for the Air Force Global Strike Command, responsible for two-thirds of the United States nuclear capabilities and arsenal. In total, Robin "Baba" Rand served on active duty for more than forty years and stayed married to Kim throughout his entire career (this is extremely rare and says something about their marriage). Anyone who served with Robin or under his leadership would attest that he was one of the greatest leaders to have ever lived. Having the opportunity to work, collaborate, and exchange thoughts with Robin on a regular basis, I too would say he's one of the greats.

Robin's Takeaways

1. Desirable Traits for Leaders

Robin believes that to be a successful leader, human being, or GAP practitioner, Robin believes people first need to understand what some of the most desirable traits of a leader are. Robin shared a few of the most desirable traits and actions he looks for in leaders.

- *Being Bold and Courageous*: One becomes bold and courageous through showing the ability to take reasonable risks with confidence and the moral strength to face danger and difficulty. And by being willing to professionally speak truth to power.
- *Holding People Accountable*: People and organizations want leaders who are clear with their expectations, hold their team members to those standards, and enforce them when they are not met.
- *Creating a Sense of Belonging*: People want to *feel* like they belong to a team and a mission that is bigger than themselves, and they value a leader who takes time to engage with them to demonstrate and articulate the value in what each individual contributor is bringing to the greater mission.
- *Humility*: Part of humility is deflecting credit to others and taking responsibility for errors, mishaps, and

mistakes. People appreciate humility over arrogance in leaders they follow. Robin kept saying throughout our interview, "Be less of what you are and work at being more of what you're not." He was indicating that it is important for leaders to try and be better at areas they've identified as weaknesses while maintaining steady growth on their existing strengths. You can't focus on being more of what you're not if you are not humble.

- *Being a Good Communicator*: Oral communication, written communication, and listening are three components of what Robin describes as important for leaders. As a good communicator, are you just transmitting? Or are you transmitting, receiving, and retaining?
- *Vulnerability*: This is not a negative term when it comes to leadership. It's demonstrating that you are willing to be uncomfortable at times and to be in positions where you are required to be the student, even with the title of a leader. We naturally gravitate toward things we are good at and avoid the things we are not good at...which can be a bad thing for quality leadership longevity.
- *Authenticity*: Leaders need to be willing to smile and laugh at themselves. Yes, there is a time to be stone-faced and stoic, but equally, there is a time to engage in humor. It shows you are human and not a robot.
- *Balance*: Instead of trying to be a high performer in just one area of your life, try to have balance and be good in your personal life as well as your professional life.

Self-awareness is the foundation for other components of awareness, according to Robin.

And if you prioritize maintaining a healthy level of self-awareness, situational, social, and sensory awareness will follow, in addition to your ability to better understand what will influence your gravitas and how well you are maintaining presence when it matters most. While Robin shared some of his most desirable traits in a leader, he continuously emphasized his belief that every trait, action, and component of GAP doesn't come naturally; they need to be continuously studied, practiced, learned, and applied, then repeated. Through the transfer of knowledge or by hard knocks, Robin swears GAP can continuously be improved.

2. The Power of Your Own Will

"In combat, we had a lot of low moments," Robin said. "The lowest moments you have in combat are when you have people on your team that are severely injured or wounded or die. As a leader of personnel who die, the road you have to go down after that is never easy; the mission could have been potentially jeopardized, you have to notify other leaders and the families of the fallen, you have to write difficult letters to loved ones, all while the mission does not stop. You don't have the luxury of taking a time-out like you can when someone dies in training, because in combat, you do not stop. While I have never claimed to be a great leader, reflecting on my career as an AF officer, I believe I was at my personal best, and my greatest GAP, when we were at our lowest as a team because *I willed myself to be at my best*. If we weren't, more deaths could happen or we could jeopardize the mission, so through the years of experience and preparation leading up to those important moments, I felt I was intentionally equipped enough to *will* myself to be strong and have impeccable GAP because my team needed that from their leader.

"Every time we lost a team member, we would bring in all the necessary leaders and component leaders. I would wait for all of them to be assembled in a room, and once they were, I would intentionally walk in, sit at the head of the table, take a few moments to look at as many people around the room in the eyes as I could. I could see their loss; I could see the heavy emotions that came with losing a close friend and teammate. I knew the importance of projecting confidence and steadfastness so my team members could take time to mourn but never lose focus of the job we had to do because we were in combat, and the alternative was more death and defeat. We could not let those who were counting on us to achieve mission success down."

3. **Prioritize Critiquing Yourself**

Throughout Robin's military career, he realized that despite having some trusted advisers who were always willing to share personal feedback with him, nobody could authentically critique himself better than he could. So, a few times each week, Robin would set aside twenty minutes with no distractions just to ask himself, *How did I do today?* and *What could I have done better?* This simple action allowed him to hold himself accountable to whether he was giving it his best or had fallen short. In other words, he was regularly increasing his self-awareness through self-reflection. Robin said, "If I only counted on other truth tellers to give me feedback and never on myself, then I would always miss out on components of feedback I needed to hear. And the feedback I needed to hear often came from myself."

4. **Personal Well-Being**

Robin said, "I had a close confidant candidly tell me, 'Boss, I greatly admire you and your passion for the mission, our airmen, and their families, and you are almost always on, except for when you're tired.'" After Robin's Cinco de Mayo party, he reprioritized his personal well-being habits as he promised his teammates. From that date forward, he tried his best to begin his formal working day no earlier than

7:30 a.m. and conclude it by 5:00 p.m. Of course, that
didn't mean he never worked outside those hours or that
he didn't sometimes take work home with him, but he knew
his gravitas and effect on others would either reflect bad
personal well-being habits or quality and sustainable ones.

Sleep became a priority for Robin, and he began to
try to get seven to eight hours every night. Sometimes an
all-nighter was required, but most of the time, he got enough
sleep to perform at his best. The alternative? Get little sleep
and continue to perform at poor levels; that wasn't good for
his performance or his teams. He shared that diet, exercise,
nutrition, sleep, education, and relationships are all things
we can take for granted but that must be prioritized. They
enable us to perform at our best and deliver stellar GAP
developments for ourselves and our teams.

Balancing GAP Takeaway

No one is going to be more critical of yourself than yourself. Self-
reflection is a core component in furthering your self-awareness. By
incorporating regular self-reflection you can enhance your awareness to influence your presence and gravitas.

FIRST WACO, NOW THIS?
Gary Noesner, Chief of the FBI's Crisis Negotiation Unit and Hostage Negotiator

Gary had just been told he was to be the Federal Bureau of Investigation's (FBI) negotiator to support the Lucasville prison riot in southern Ohio in 1993. The day he was told to get on a plane to Ohio, he saw the Waco fire unfolding live on TV news stations. Gary had been the FBI's lead negotiator for the first half of the Waco siege and found himself having to reset his focus and prepare for the next scenario.

Throughout Gary's thirty-year career as an investigator, instructor, and negotiator, he was exposed to hundreds of crisis situations that required his gravitas, awareness, and presence; lives often depended on it. For twenty-three years at the FBI, he was primarily a hostage negotiator, retiring as chief of the FBI's Crisis Negotiation Unit, Critical Incident Response Group. As the first person to hold that position, he was heavily involved in numerous crisis incidents covering prison riots, militia standoffs, religious zealot sieges, terrorist embassy takeovers, airplane hijackings, and over 120 overseas kidnapping cases involving American citizens.

When Gary arrived in Ohio, he felt sharp as he transitioned his focus from Waco to the Lucasville prison riot. Gary joined the prison's team—who up until this point had been "handling" the situation. As always, Gary's first act was to gain situational awareness of the environment as well as social and sensory awareness of the team who knew the prisoners. On Easter Sunday, more than four hundred inmates at the correctional facility had taken over a prison block, resulting in the death of one guard and nine inmates. Certain inmates sparked the riot because they did not want to receive a tuberculosis test that required an injection containing alcohol, saying it would violate their religious views.

Gary immediately assessed that the prison's team was exhausted, angry because one of their own had been killed, and in total chaos. The team looked to Gary to take over the situation; they knew he was one of the primary negotiators at Waco, and therefore his gravitas radiated to the prison team: He was experienced, had a lot of exposure to more intense environments than this one, and had just been engaged in another high-tension scenario. Assessing this through his awareness, Gary intentionally maintained a calm and collected sense of gravitas and physical demeanor as he asked the prison team some questions.

Self-aware of his exhaustion after giving full attention to Waco over the past weeks, Gary received information and quickly learned that the inmates were taking turns at getting on the phone and making demands to the prison's team: money, a plane to South America, girlfriends to be brought to the prison, and so on. The prison team was frustrated because there was no singular prisoner identifying as the leader of the riot, so the inmates' demands were not aligned.

Through inquiry and facilitation, Gary got the prison team to agree on the value of getting the prison inmates organized. Gary had the prison team negotiator call and tell the inmates that they needed to identify a leader to have thoughtful discussions. The inmates obliged and selected three leaders, one from each of the large gangs in the prison. The inmate leaders and the prison team's leadership met in the yard with a barbed-wire chain-link fence separating the two, and they began discussions. After the meeting, the prison team brought twenty inmate requests to Gary and said, "We can't do all of this. These demands are ridiculous." Gary asked the prison team to read the demands carefully because he thought they could say yes to all of them. The twenty requests were just that—requests. Not demands, requests. For example, one of the requests was, "You will try to get better food in the canteen." Legally, they did not have to fulfill any request, but Gary valued the fact that the inmates were not demanding an outcome, they were demanding a process. The prison team agreed to the inmates' requests and the riot ended. Mission accomplished.

Gary's Takeaways

1. **Emotional Regulation (Awareness)**

   As a crisis negotiator for the FBI, Gary saw, interacted with, and frequently engaged people on the other end of the phone who had lost their emotional control. During our interview, Gary reminded me that often when emotions are high, rational thinking is low. When it comes to GAP, maintaining emotional composure regardless of the environment, or at least being aware of your emotional responses, is important in maintaining self-awareness and gravitas.

When you are on the receiving end of someone who has lost their emotional composure, you must recognize that you cannot control their actions, but you can influence them based on your response.

2. **Demeanor and Voice (Gravitas and Presence)**

Despite Hollywood scenes depicting crisis negotiations, Gary knows from experience that in a negotiation situation, an authoritative voice with a demand is almost never the right approach. People want to feel respected, and they want you to be sincere, genuine, and authentic. When trying to reach a positive outcome with another human through your interactions, lead with being thoughtful and showing them respect.

People are comfortable when they speak about themselves, their journey, and their experiences. By engaging with others through the lens of seeking to understand them, asking thoughtful questions about themselves and their experiences, you can deescalate a tense environment and put people in a comfortable mindset. When Gary joined the prison team, his first action was to assess the environment, and his second was to ask questions to better understand what had taken place.

Crisis negotiators must maintain a hyperfocused presence because every single detail exchanged could be a clue or indication of motive or a potential resolution. Negotiators are trained to minimize distractions so they can focus on nothing but the words being used, tone of voice, and emotions expressed by the person on the other end of the line. If you put the same focus on your presence in human interactions into action, what takeaways would you draw?

3. **Environment (Awareness)**

Visualization, paired with a probability matrix of likelihood versus unlikelihood, assists in situational awareness. When Gary showed up to support the prison team's negotiators, they weren't having success with the rotation of inmates getting on the phone and making demands. Gary visualized the environment of the inmate making the call; he was probably in front of his fellow inmates acting tougher than he was. This provided Gary with a context that the inmates did not want to seem less than alpha in front of their fellow inmates, so they were putting on a show while on the phone with the prison negotiators and acting tougher than they actually were or were intending to be. As a solution, Gary proposed that when the inmates identify their leaders, they come out into the yard to meet with the prison team. This way, the inmates did not have to save face in front of the other inmates and could instead focus on getting to an authentic solution. The environment you are in, and the environment others are in, often influences attitudes, decisions, outcomes, and pressures. With situational awareness and visualization, one can identify the environments and their potential influences to better strategize on a third option.

Balancing GAP Takeaway

Experience, knowledge, and intentionality are all required throughout the journey of mastering your GAP. Emotional regulation will always assist you in performing at your best in each of the three GAP categories.

BECOMING PARTNER AT MCKINSEY IN FIVE YEARS
Bill O'Keefe, Partner at McKinsey and Company

*R*oughly eighteen months into his job as an associate at McKinsey and Company, the world's premier management consulting firm, Bill had just wrapped up leading a client collaboration session when his project manager asked to speak with him in private afterward. "Bill, you don't always need to be so assertive and dominant in these client sessions. The client knows we're smart, but they need to be heard, and for them to be heard, we need to give them the opportunity to contribute thoughts about their business. Yes, we improve organizational efficiencies, help solve problems, and increase our list of clients' performance throughout the globe so we have unique perspective, but oftentimes, the client knows their specific business better than we can, and we need to hear from them." For Bill, this was a turning point.

Bill grew up in Minnesota and received a bachelor's degree in English and history. He excelled at his first job in the private sector for reinsurance intermediary Benfield for seven years, then decided to pursue an MBA. With grit and tenacity, Bill earned his MBA at the Tuck School of Business at Dartmouth and then immediately joined McKinsey. Walking into McKinsey every day created anxiety, self-doubt, and overwhelming thoughts of being an impostor. Bill was different; he did not grow up privileged or attend a premier undergraduate university. Soon Bill's anxiety and self-doubt created small bouts of depression and caused many sleepless nights. Bill took on the mindset of having to show everyone in the office that he belonged at McKinsey, and his method for doing so was being assertive and the most knowledgeable person at the table...or so he thought.

When Bill's project manager shared the feedback with him that he needed to improve as a collaborator who could provoke questions and seek understanding instead of just asserting the answers and knowledge, this was an *aha* moment for Bill. Following the feedback he received, Bill prioritized improving his self-awareness, specifically by being more aware of how his colleagues and clients perceived him in interactions. After consistent daily reflection, Bill came up with a technique for self-accountability that he calls the 70/30 rule. 70 percent of the time he would interact with a client, he would do so by asking questions, influencing collaboration, and seeking understanding. The remaining 30 percent of the time, he would share his knowledge and contributions to the discussion. By always saying to himself "70/30" before going into a client or internal team interaction, he enhanced his presence and ability to follow his 70/30 guideline. At the end of each day, Bill would reflect on his day's performance and give himself a grade on whether he did well or needed to improve the next day. Bill quickly learned that not only were his interactions with others becoming better, but the end results, products, and solutions they were producing for their clients were improving too because he'd created space for increased involvement and collaboration.

A few weeks after implementing his 70/30 rule, Bill was invited to join other McKinsey associates for an off-site retreat led by expert leadership development facilitators. Bill recalled this as his second big *aha* moment as an associate. Through third-party facilitated sessions, Bill learned that almost every single McKinsey associate there was also struggling with anxiety and impostor syndrome. On the flight home, Bill couldn't stop thinking that his increased awareness of other team members within McKinsey meant he could create more unified teams by leveraging a vulnerability that nearly everybody was experiencing but no one had spoken about. Accepting that everyone is human and carries their own self-doubt or limiting beliefs, Bill arrived at work the next day with more confidence. This increase in his awareness heightened his confidence and presence, accelerating his ability to perform.

After five years at McKinsey, Bill was named partner with a specialization in strategy. Only 1 percent of those who apply to McKinsey are hired. Of that 1 percent, only one out of sixteen make partner, and of those who do, only one in three do so within five years (the fastest possible track to become a partner at the firm). So, after two *aha* moments within his first eighteen months at the firm, how did he enhance, increase, and accelerate his gravitas, awareness, and presence over the next three and a half years to make partner? Bill shares his playbook in his takeaways below.

Bill's Takeaways

1. **Your Focus Should Almost Always Be Communication**
   In business and perhaps life, communication is one of the single most valuable differentiators, according to Bill. Too often, people in business are focused on the "what": *What are we selling? What makes people want to buy it? What information is necessary to share with the client?* and the list goes on. But Bill says people should focus more on the *how* and *why*

when communicating. Yes, the *what* is important, but the how and why are where you can create an experience for the individual(s) you are communicating with. Bill describes communication as theater; it should be thoroughly thought about, researched, and rehearsed, creating a unique experience for those on the receiving end.

Before Bill goes into a client proposal delivery or strategic meeting, he conducts as much intelligence gathering as he can on the people who will be in the room to receive his message. Here is an example list of what Bill asks himself while preparing for an important exchange: *How do I want people to feel? How do I get them excited? Which people in the room will be key influencers when I am not in the room, and how do I want them to feel? What are the individual concerns, priorities, and motivations of the individuals in the room? What are the organization's concerns, priorities, and motivations?* When Bill feels like he has exhausted all the time, energy, and resources he can on answering those questions, he has a foundation to begin planning his communication performance.

Awareness is understanding the answers to the above questions and contexts. Gravitas comes when you've become aware enough to prepare to communicate, and those on the receiving end are left with a feeling of wanting to partner with you.

2. **Remember Each Phase of Your Career Progression**
Making partner in five years at the world's premier management consulting firm is no small accomplishment. As Bill progressed in his career, leading others as a senior associate, manager, and partner, he never forgot the feelings and emotions he had as a new associate at the firm. Intentionally, Bill would find opportunities to connect with his direct reports individually and through informal team gatherings, such as team dinners, to lead with vulnerability and share the feelings and emotions he once experienced as an

associate (and occasionally still does as a partner!). Creating psychologically safe environments for his team members to hear the reality of how the firm can sometimes make people feel only enhanced his gravitas as an empathetic and thoughtful leader among his direct reports.

McKinsey regularly executed formal evaluations during and at the end of each client project for both the client and for the McKinsey team to complete. McKinsey team members rated their leader in categories like inspiration, learning, and leading. This created a continuous loop for partners to receive direct feedback from those they were leading on every product, and at the end of the year, team evaluations held massive weight on the partner's annual review. Bill continuously ranked in the top percentile of North American partners, and he attributes much of his success in leading others to understanding where they were mentally and emotionally, based on experiencing the very same states when he was in the same position. The big difference between him and other partners with the same experiences and career progression was that Bill prioritized speaking with his team members about it. This disarming and vulnerable approach could have been perceived as an interruption of a McKinsey partner's gravitas, but it actually enhanced his gravitas with those he was leading.

3. Be Authentic Early, Not Later

As Bill has progressed in his career, he has experienced first-hand and observed from others how to become successful at creating meaningful relationships (something Bill and anyone else who is successful in business knows in one of the most important contributions to success). Whether socially or professionally, he believes it is critically important to be authentic as soon as possible with people—quite literally to be yourself. While this may seem obvious to many, Bill has observed that many people will put on an inauthentic persona when meeting someone for the first time, or remain overly reserved in what could be perceived as sharing too much personal information about yourself with someone you've only just met. They become truly authentic and more like themselves only after meeting several more times, getting to know someone better, or spending lots of time together.

Through lived experience and observation, Bill believes the better way is to be completely authentic and yourself as soon as possible. People want to do business or have relationships with people they like, can relate to, can trust, can admire, and can be human with, not just a professional robot. If you are seeking a competitive advantage over others when attempting to win over a prospective client, be yourself. When you are attempting to establish a relationship with someone for the first time, be yourself. Nothing is more refreshing than others feeling like they got to know the real you and not just a professional front.

Underscoring the importance of being authentic and being authentic early, Bill made sure to point out there is so much value in this takeaway for leaders interacting with their own team members. If your team knows you are a trustworthy, good person who is doing your best to be authentic and do the right thing, they will work harder and have more confidence in following you. And if the business environment becomes challenging and you are faced with tough decisions or critical conversations, those will be easier because at least your team members know who you are and that whatever tough decisions or updates you must share are, at the very least, originating from a good place.

Authenticity is easy when you lean into the categories of self-, situational, social, and sensory awareness. It may

be counterintuitive to some but not to Bill: Authenticity
enhances gravitas.

4. Leaders Are Obligated to Give Feedback

During our interview, Bill reflected on a leadership class he
took as part of his MBA studies at Tuck. Despite not thoroughly enjoying the class itself, Bill was left with a piece of
wisdom from his professor that he has never forgotten. Bill's
leadership professor said, "As a leader, your job is not to
be liked by those you are leading. Your job is to help those
you are leading reach their full potential." Bill still strives
to be liked but remembers that statement when he gives
critical or uncomfortable counsel. He believes he has an
obligation to share feedback with those on his team, especially when he is leading them. They might not like to hear
it, but it's an obligation of a leader. If you're lucky, one day
when they mature and their business tenure increases, they
will remember you as a leader who cared and helped them
reach their full potential.

When giving feedback, Bill tries to avoid vagueness or
generalities like, "That was a really great presentation in
there." Instead, Bill focuses on giving specific feedback that
highlights a specific example where he observed a team
member do well or do not so well. By avoiding generic feedback, you provide your team member a specific example
that they can reflect on, ask questions about, and use as a
model to methodically walk through their logic, thinking,
and internal dialogue. This allows you as a leader to assist
your team members in enhancing their awareness and
growing their gravitas.

Balancing GAP Takeaway

Bill's meteoric rise within McKinsey, one of the world's most
competitive professional services firms, illustrates how embracing
and adjusting your gravitas, awareness, and presence works in

real time and how educating, experimenting, and evaluating only strengthens it over the years.

PART 3

PUTTING GAP
INTO ACTION

CHAPTER 6

THE PLAYBOOK

I believe that self-awareness and the three other awareness components are crucial to leadership and having successful relationships with others. My personal theory is that GAP differentiates those who are good in their profession from those who are great. Once you start building the foundation of GAP, so many other things come out of it. Perhaps you've seen this in action in the case studies you've just read.

It reminds me of the lessons I learned from my "peanut butter jelly sandwich" incident when I was eighteen years old and in training to become a Navy SEAL. As I shared at the beginning of this book, I lacked awareness; I did not understand how others perceived me and my actions, and it was very different from how I perceived myself and my actions. Just one minor adjustment, joining them for peanut butter and jelly sandwiches instead of sleeping, led to a turnaround. Though this experience might seem small and somewhat comical, this simple misunderstanding and lack of awareness could have resulted in the instructors removing me from training because I wasn't rated high enough in the peer evaluations. The experience immediately humbled me and prompted me to prioritize enhancing my GAP from that day forward.

I have since separated from the military, and now I have been in business much longer than I had served, but based on what I learned there, I have prioritized being a student of GAP. I'd gone from a career as a Navy SEAL, what many would acknowledge is one of the best military units in the world, to entering business, and it transitioned me from being an "expert" in my craft to once again being a beginner. Fortunately, I had enough self-awareness through my transition to identify what I was confident and competent in and where I needed to learn. And over time, that developed into GAP and the Gap Enhancement Cycle I now share and implement with those I coach.

I have observed some of the highest-performing business professionals practicing elements of what became the GAP Enhancement Cycle, and science proves it is a competitive advantage. My curiosity from my observations gradually expanded as I began coaching global executives and going through executive education programs at Harvard Business School. During our coaching sessions, one of the first things I would ask is, "What areas would you like to prioritize improving during our coaching sessions?" Almost every time, they would respond with wanting to increase elements of their gravitas, awareness, and presence. Multiply this by the thousands of executives I have had the privilege of working alongside, and it was clear the need was quite serious. Leaders, professionals, and learners were identifying GAP as something people talked about, wanted, and expected from their leadership, yet they did not know where to get it or how to develop it. This, paired with my own curiosity and experience, motivated me to create a resource that could answer the voids surrounding GAP. The science and the practitioner examples I've shared with you in this book allow you to not just intellectually understand GAP but also internalize how it is used in action.

In a world where academics challenge practitioners to back up their positions and beliefs with data, and practitioners challenge academics to put their theory into practice, this is a resource that answers both calls to action.

In this book, you have reviewed the scientific data surrounding the elements of GAP in action and what impact they can have on your individual and team performance. You've also reviewed world-class leadership practitioners' lived experiences and learned from times when they had or did not have GAP. These practitioners have different experiences, live in different places, and are in different industries. Yet each of them had a story to share about how they've continued learning to master their own GAP to elevate their individual and team performance.

Like anything, knowledge is useless without application. So now it's your turn. It is time to apply your newly gained knowledge. First, I challenge you to apply (when applicable and appropriate) many of the takeaways shared with you by the world-class practitioners. To do that, let's revisit the building blocks of GAP.

Having read through the case studies and research in this book, what do the terms *gravitas, awareness,* and *presence* mean to you?

You'll remember my definitions from the beginning of this journey:

Gravitas is the influence, emotions, and feelings someone's demeanor evokes in others.

Awareness is composed of what I like to call SA4:

- Self-Awareness: The perception of self being aligned with the perception of others
- Situational Awareness: Understanding the context and details of an event or action
- Social Awareness: Understanding of the context and details of an exchange between two or more people, often determined by the environment
- Sensory Awareness: The sensory responses (emotion, voice changes, body position, eye contact, etc.) to a situation or event

Presence is the state of being in mental, emotional, social, and charismatic forms.

Next, we revisit the **GAP Enhancement Cycle** to explore how these elements balance each other.

GAP Enhancement Cycle

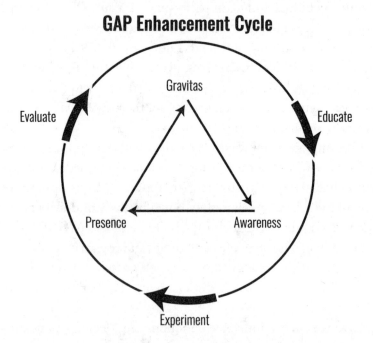

This illustration shows how gravitas, awareness, and presence are interdependent. They amplify each other, and if someone is lacking in one of the three, chances are, the other two are suffering.

You'll notice how GAP Enhancement Cycle has a continuous, outer circle that progresses from *educate* to *experiment* to *evaluate*.

- **Educate** reflects a thorough understanding of what GAP is and how to build it.
- **Experiment** is your next step, where you will put this knowledge and understanding into action as a practitioner.
- **Evaluate** involves debriefing and reflecting on what went well and what could have gone better in the experiment phase.

When the educate, experiment, evaluate circle is put into action, you can continuously cycle through the phases for ongoing development and growth of your GAP, ultimately increasing your GAP through every complete rotation.

YOUR OWN GAP ENHANCEMENT CYCLE

Now, let's apply each part of the cycle to your situation.

Educate

Reading this book, you have already begun the **educate** piece of the GAP Enhancement Cycle. How will you continue your education? I suggest seeking additional perspectives and understandings of GAP. Some quality resources can be found in podcasts, TED talks, academic papers, and from thought leaders on the domains of gravitas, awareness, and presence. You can explore books, formal education programs, and executive coaches, and, of course, you can actively become a GAP practitioner using the tools outlined in this book.

Experiment

As you continue to learn new information on the topic of GAP, try and put those ideas into action through experiments when appropriate. For example, I wouldn't suggest putting a new learning into action for the first time during a high-stakes meeting or professional opportunity. Instead, try and identify opportunities where you can put your new learnings into action for the first time that have a low risk if the implementation does not turn out how you would have hoped. GAP experiments often turn out best in low-risk environments that are psychologically safe, enabling you to try something without serious repercussions if it doesn't provide the impact you hoped for. Think of each of these experiments as an opportunity to engage in a GAP Enhancement Cycle repetition, knowing you will evaluate it afterward. Think of these GAP experiments as repetitions, helping you gain awareness on whether a technique or methodology worked for you or needs to be adjusted and improved. Whether you are just beginning your professional career or you are a seasoned veteran of industry, GAP repetitions and experiments will *always* assist you in enhancing your GAP, ultimately preparing you for your next level.

Evaluate

Following each GAP experiment, be disciplined in consistent evaluation. The best teams and individual practitioners in any sport, business, or professional domain regularly incorporate evaluations after every practice or live event. Often referred to as debriefs or after-actions, these evaluations are opportunities to identify lessons. Once lessons are identified, they can be applied, and the cycle starts over. After you engage in a GAP experiment, make time immediately following the experiment, if you can, to assess the performance of the experiment and its implications, faults, and areas for improvement.

When in the *evaluate* stage, leaders can sometimes make the mistake of asking "why" when they should be asking "what": "*Why* did this happen?" versus "*What* did I do to make this happen?" An example of this would be if you were to get notified you did not win a big client opportunity with your proposal. Instead of looking just externally and asking, *Why did this happen?* there is value in first asking, *What did I do to make this happen or what did I not do that influenced this result?* Asking just *why* can drive us to get stuck in hypotheticals, interpretations, and imagination, whereas using the basis of *what* allows a leader to focus on the facts of an interaction or evaluation. Simply asking *why* can create facts that do not exist. Focusing on the *whats* will lead you to better understand factual information instead of hypothetical information.

REFLECT ON YOUR GAP: QUESTIONS FOR
SELF-ASSESSMENT AND UNDERSTANDING

To get your GAP Enhancement Cycle going, start with a practice of self-awareness. Below I have categorized some practitioner tools and exercises to assist you in using specific techniques in addition to all that was shared by the world-class practitioners in their stories. We'll dig into each category of GAP and explore how you can implement changes in your life. Let's begin with a step-by-step guide for how to apply *awareness* in your daily life.

AWARENESS

Self-Awareness

These questions can be a starting point of understanding of your own self-awareness. Take some time to journal and reflect in order to know yourself better.

- What are your values?
- What three words would you use to describe yourself, and why did you choose those terms?
- What three words does your spouse or a loved one use to describe you, and why (in their words and with their reason for choosing those words)?
- What three words does your closest professional colleague use to describe you, and why (in their words and with their reason for choosing those words)?
- How often do you analyze how a human interaction will go before engaging with that person? And when you do, what is your thought process to analyze hypothetical interactions before they happen?
- How often do you debrief interactions with others? And when you do, how do you do it? If you do not do it, seek some information on debrief methodologies and guidance so that you can begin debriefing.
- Is there someone you can think of who embodies the following: *When they enter the room, people can feel it.* How would you describe what their gravitas brings to the room that was not there before?

- Do you believe you can change how you are perceived based on the environment you are operating within? Why or why not?
- How would your family describe your presence at home?
- How would your team and clients describe your presence at work?
- Create a "mission statement" for your life that describes why you are on this earth.
- Take a look at the Self-Awareness Matrix below. Where do you land on the matrix? Where would your colleagues say you land on the matrix? Where would you like to land?

THE MASTERING YOUR GAP SELF-AWARENESS MATRIX

Perception of Self (High)	**The Fossil** They know who they are but don't have the motivation to adapt, change, or be open to feedback from others. Stuck in their ways, this limits their ability to foster professional relationships and can limit their success. Often, the aware-don't-care can fall into this category.	**The Self-Aware** They understand who they are, what they believe, and what their guiding principles are. They regularly seek feedback from others and reflect on their own words, actions, and body language. This often positively influences their individual and team performance.
(Low)	**The Not Self-Aware** They don't know who they are or what their values and belief system is yet. They lack an understanding of self and how others perceive them. This may lead to a lack of performance and an inability to develop relationships.	**The Chameleon** They don't have a strong understanding of who they are yet. They adapt, change, and can potentially think like the environment or culture they are immersed in without having a clear understanding of what it is they believe. This may lead them to make choices that are not to their benefit.

Perception of Others — Low → High

Situational Awareness

Now that you've reflected and begun the journey of increasing your self-awareness, take these tools into your next meeting or planned professional interaction and explore how awareness of the situation can enhance your experience, performance, and outcomes.

Before entering a new room or environment, ask yourself:

- Who will be there?
- What will the environment look like?
- What energy could be in the environment?
- How do I want to be perceived?
- Am I wearing the right clothes?
- What knowledge or topics do I want to be aware of?
- Have any events occurred that could influence the interactions of those in this environment? If so, what should I be ready for?
- How can I gain the best understanding of the environment before entering it?

Once you enter a new room or environment, try to observe the following:

- Who is here?
- Who do I know, and who do I not know?
- Which interactions between others look comfortable or uncomfortable? Why do I think that is?
- Is there someone here whom people are gravitating toward?
- Is there someone here whom people are avoiding?
- How is this environment different than I imagined it would be?
- What surprises me?
- What disappoints me?
- How can I maximize my time and effort here?
- How do others perceive me?

When you leave the room or environment, ask yourself:
- How did that go?
- How did I come across to those I interacted with?
- How do I think people who saw me interacting with others perceived me?
- If I were to receive a do-over in that environment, what would I do differently?
- What stood out as peculiar?

Social Awareness

Before going into a social environment, ask yourself:
- What is the intent of this event?
- How can the political, economic, or current events impact these exchanges?
- Does this event have a theme?
- What is appropriate for me to wear based on the theme and intent of the event?
- Are there subsegments of people in this environment who have a history of rapport? If so, what is it, and how important is it to each of them?

Sensory Awareness

The following questions apply in one-on-one interactions as well as group interactions.

When engaging in discussion with another person, ask yourself:
- Are they making eye contact with me?
- Is their body language positive (facing me, leaning in, focused) or negative (turned away from me, disinterested)?
- How is their tone of voice (angry, sad, anxious, concerned, happy, enthusiastic)?
- Are they showing any heartfelt emotional gestures toward me?
- Are they looking at their watch or their phone while engaging with me?

By engaging in some of these awareness practices, reflections, and resources, you are already on your way to furthering your awareness and setting a strong foundation for the remaining components of GAP—presence and gravitas.

PRESENCE

Here are a few tips that can assist to enhance your presence with humans and with tasks.

- Know yourself! If you get easily sidetracked, get creative with what you can incorporate into your schedule to minimize distraction and enhance your presence. For example:
  - Remove your smartwatch so you're not tempted to look at it frequently.
  - Use the "do not disturb" option on your smartphone and devices before and during your meetings with others or when doing important tasks.
- Allocate a few minutes before every virtual or in-person meeting to mentally and emotionally "detach" from what may have occurred before your meeting, and center yourself for your next engagement from a neutral, uninfluenced state of mind.
- Consistently schedule time to refresh, recharge, and rehydrate.
- Use a pen and paper when engaging with others; when a thought comes to mind and you don't want it to distract you or negatively influence your presence, quickly write down something that will remind you of that thought and then return your focus to optimize your presence.

GRAVITAS

As shown throughout this book, you need to be a consistent practitioner of awareness and presence in order to positively influence your gravitas. Here are some additional thoughts to remind you how to influence your gravitas for the better.

- Credibility comes from a demonstrated track record of success, perseverance, motivation, competence, awareness, and presence.
- The reputation you establish as a person will always influence your gravitas.
- The more experience, wisdom, insight, and knowledge you gain, the more confidence you will experience, and that competence will radiate when engaging with others.
- Specific roles, responsibilities, and job titles influence gravitas perceived by others.
- The organization you are a part of carries its own influences, reputation, and perceptions that, through your association as an employee or team member, can influence your gravitas.

While not all-encompassing, the questions, reflections, and observations listed above will provide a methodical progression of reflection points to enhance your GAP before, during, and after opportunities for experiments. Though this all may seem relatively simple, the challenge lies in the consistency of *doing*. Simply, do.

People often believe that intelligence equals complexity, especially when they're thinking about growing gravitas, awareness, and presence in a professional setting. I would argue that the greatest form of intelligence can sometimes equal simplicity. Take Google, for example: a simple page with a white backdrop, their name displayed, and a search bar. It's so simple, yet it leads users to the most complex informational database in the world. In the same way, keep your experiments and reflections simple to start, and as you accelerate in your repetitions, they may become more complex.

To simplify, add balance. Use the following image as a visual reminder that too much or too little of one component of GAP can cause adverse reactions or consequences with the other two.

Therefore, it is important that you try and be equally balanced in all three components of GAP.

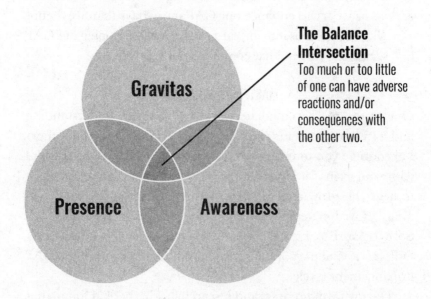

The Balance Intersection
Too much or too little of one can have adverse reactions and/or consequences with the other two.

After researching GAP for close to a decade and reviewing more than sixty years of research, I consider it important to warn you that negative consequences can arise when someone becomes obsessive with developing their own GAP. So I feel responsible to share with you a reminder that we are all human and should give ourselves grace as we navigate enhancing our GAP. Becoming obsessive with the GAP Enhancement Cycle without giving yourself some grace can result in paranoia, overanalysis, and exhaustion from never recognizing how much you've improved—especially when you're primarily focusing on where you could improve next time. We can try to maintain continuous awareness on a consistent basis, yet there are certainly times when other things and actions should be prioritized over the methodical progression of the GAP Enhancement Cycle techniques. I will be the first to tell you that despite being an academic researcher on the topic of

GAP and trying to be a regular practitioner of a well-balanced GAP, I am not perfect, and I can always do better than I am. The key is investing in knowledge and aligning our intentions with our actions as we try to enhance our GAP more days than we do not. This should propel us into forward progress in developing our GAP and seeing the success that comes from it.

MASTERING *YOUR* GAP

One of the most immediate ways you can seek understanding and awareness on your GAP is by seeking feedback from others. I encourage you to first seek out those you know will be truthful with you, even if it is hard to hear, because they genuinely want to help you grow and develop. As humans, even the most self-aware of us don't enjoy hearing critical feedback about ourselves. So it is hard to approach feedback regularly and consistently. Still, it is a vital part of the *evaluation* component within the GAP Enhancement Cycle.

During my interviews and research for this book, I found that those who had the highest levels of self-awareness didn't often immediately act on critical feedback they received from others. Instead, they thoughtfully processed the feedback they received over a few days, or sometimes even weeks before making a decision on how they would implement a change or improvement. I encourage you to make the most of the feedback you receive by finding a methodology for evaluation and implementation that works best for you.

Gravitas, awareness, and presence assist us in living more thoughtful, methodical, intentional, and maximized lives—in our work environments, as parents, in our relationships, and especially with leading ourselves and others. To love ourselves, we first need to know ourselves, or else we just love the idea of ourselves. After receiving thoughtful feedback from close friends and colleagues on my first book, *Leadership A Life Sport: A Playbook on What It Takes to Win as an Individual and as a Team*, I wanted to cover the topic of

GAP in my next book to elevate the reader experience even further. I've never been a fan of books that are simply "how-to" books. How could one formula or solution be applicable to every individual's circumstances? It's not. I wrote *Mastering Your G.A.P.* to be a resource for those seeking scientific data, research, knowledge, real-world examples of GAP in action, and I hope you'll use these playbook applications to implement immediate methodologies to enhance your own GAP. Most importantly, I wanted you as the reader to join me and our practitioner contributors on a learning journey and to reach a place of deep thought and reflection. I hope this book has given you the tools you need to put that reflection into practice and continue leading with curiosity. You would not have started this journey to better understand GAP if you were not a curious person. Continue to always try and expand your depth of thought and ability to think. Use that curiosity to propel yourself forward, and go master your GAP!

ACKNOWLEDGMENTS

My writing journey has continued since writing my first book, *Leadership A Life Sport*. To all those throughout the world that I have crossed paths with on this journey, I thank you; there is not enough space in this book to include all of you, but I have learned something from each of you.

As it relates to this book in particular, I do have specific people to thank. To my team at Victory Strategies, thank you for your belief in me and our mission. You teach me every single day. To Joshua Margolis, thank you for believing in me, betting on me, and teaching me. Working alongside you as an Executive Fellow at Harvard Business School is one of the greatest honors of my life. And to all of those who have agreed to be interviewed and included in this book, sharing personal and invaluable lessons of your GAP experience with the world: Scott Campbell, Ted DeZabala, Chris Brown, Jennifer Walsh, Lauren Crandall, Jason Lamb, Jerry Morgan, Samantha Weeks, Anne Marie Jess Hansen, Dan Cockerell, Gary Noesner, Rod Fox, Jeff Boyer, Jessica Buchanan, Robert Schleusner, Diana Markaki-Bartholdi, Jon Cute, Chris Rubio, Christopher Brown, Justin Delaney, Gabrielle Ivey, Rabbi Rob Thomas, Robin Rand, Joe De Sena, Iván López, Joe Nunziata, Bill O'Keefe, Simon Katz, William McRaven.

Life is better when you are not alone, and I am so grateful that I am not. Without my strongest supporter, best friend, and wife, Jessie, this would not have come together. Any award, accomplishment, or milestone met would be meaningless without you to share it with. Thank you for helping me enhance my GAP every single day, being my biggest supporter, and being the greatest mother to our daughter, Thea.

ABOUT THE AUTHOR

*J*acob Werksman is the founder and CEO of Victory Strategies, an author, an Executive Fellow at Harvard Business School, and a former Navy SEAL. Jacob is regularly sought after for his presentations and speaking engagements on the topics of leadership and GAP to impact individuals and teams throughout the world.

In business, Jacob started Victory Strategies with his life savings to pursue his belief in the American dream. Victory Strategies is a leadership development, training, and coaching firm whose primary purpose is to help leaders accelerate their leadership and performance through embracing the possible. He began by assembling a world-class team of professionals from the most elite communities in the world. These leadership practitioners include Navy SEALs, *Fortune* 500 executives, Olympic athletes and coaches, TOPGUN fighter pilots, and high-performing entrepreneurs. Through other formal and informal capacities, Jacob provides strategic advisory services to several businesses and organizations throughout the world.

In academia, Jacob conducts research, collaborates, and teaches as an executive fellow at Harvard Business School (HBS), and engages in various executive education programs as an executive leadership coach to global executives throughout their time in Boston. Outside of Harvard Business School, Jacob is an adjunct professor in leadership at the University of Central Florida and has guest lectured at academic institutions throughout the world.

In the news, Jacob has been published, interviewed, or featured in *Forbes,* Fox News, the *Orlando Business Journal,* and many other outlets.

In publishing, and in addition to this book, Jacob authored *Leadership A Life Sport: A Playbook on What It Takes to Win as an Individual and as a Team* in 2020.

In the classroom, Jacob holds a bachelor's degree in organizational leadership, is an alumnus of Harvard Business School, and holds a doctorate in business administration (DBA) from the Crummer Graduate School of Business at Rollins College. Believing in the value of continuous education, Jacob has also attended executive certificate programs at the following institutions: Georgetown University, University of Oxford, Columbia University, and Harvard Business School.

In service, and prior to starting Victory Strategies, Jacob served in the United States military as a Navy SEAL. Since separating from his military service, Jacob continues his passion for giving back through active and regular charitable engagements and sits on several nonprofit boards.

Connect and learn more at www.victory-strategies.com.

NOTES

1 Lao Tzu, *Tao-te Ching,* trans. Wing-Tsit Chan, ch. 33 in
   Susan Radcliffe, ed., *Oxford Essential Quotations, 5th ed.,*
   2017, https://www.oxfordreference.com/display/10.1093/
   acref/9780191843730.001.0001/q-oro-ed5-00006490.

2 M. Showry and K. V. L. Manasa, "Self-Awareness: Key to
   Effective Leadership," *The IUP Journal of Soft Skills* 8, no. 1 (2014):
   15–26.

3 E. Van Velsor, S. Taylor, and J. B. Leslie, "An Examination
   of The Relationships Among Self-Perception Accuracy, Self-
   Awareness, Gender, and Leader Effectiveness," *Human Resource
   Management* 32, nos. 2–3 (1993): 249–63, https://doi.org/10.1002/
   hrm.3930320205.

4 Laozi and Brian Browne Walker, *The Tao TE Ching of Lao Tzu: A
   New Translation* (St. Martin's Griffin, 1996), n.p.

5 Shelley Duval and Robert A. Wicklund, *A Theory of Objective Self
   Awareness* (Academic Press, 1972).

6 Tasha Eurich, *Insight: The Surprising Truth About How Others See
   Us, How We See Ourselves, and Why the Answers Matter More Than We
   Think* (Currency, 2018).

7 Roy F. Baumeister, *The Cultural Animal: Human Nature, Meaning,
   and Social Life* (Oxford University Press, 2005).

8 Zuzana Sasovova, "To Dislike and to Be Liked: Self-Monitoring,
   Affect-Intensive Relations and Work Performance," *Academy of
   Management Proceedings* 1 (2006): 1–6, https://doi.org/10.5465/
   ambpp.2006.22898634.

9 Hsiang-Chu Pai, "The Effect of a Self-Reflection and Insight

Program on the Nursing Competence of Nursing Students: A Longitudinal Study," *Journal of Professional Nursing* 31, no. 5 (2015): 424–31, https://doi.org/10.1016/j.profnurs.2015.03.003.

10 Allan H. Church, "Managerial Self-Awareness in High-Performing Individuals in Organizations," *Journal of Applied Psychology* 82, no. 2 (1997): 281–92, https://doi.org/10.1037/0021-9010.82.2.281.

11 Duval and Wicklund, *A Theory of Objective Self Awareness*.

12 Daniel Goleman, *Emotional Intelligence* (Bloomsbury, 1995).

13 Duval and Wicklund, *A Theory of Objective Self Awareness*.

14 Duval and Wicklund, *A Theory of Objective Self Awareness*.

15 P. J. Silvia and T. S. Duval, "Objective Self-Awareness Theory: Recent Progress and Enduring Problems," *Personality and Social Psychology Review* 5, no. 3 (2001): 230–41, https://doi.org/10.1207/s15327957pspr0503_4.

16 Sasovova, "To Dislike and to Be Liked."

17 Showry and Manasa, "Self-Awareness."

18 Showry and Manasa, "Self-Awareness."

19 Scott N. Taylor, "Redefining Leader Self-Awareness by Integrating the Second Component of Self-Awareness," *Journal of Leadership Studies* 3, no. 4 (2010): 57–68, https://doi.org/10.1002/jls.20139.

20 Michael Walton, "Enhancing Executive Self-Awareness: Two Approaches for Consideration," *IUP Journal of Soft Skills* 16, no. 2 (2022): 7–15, https://www.academia.edu/119206772/Five_Perspectives_to_Enhance_Self_Understanding.

21 Ellen Van Velsor, Sylvester Taylor, and Jean B. Leslie, "An Examination of the Relationships Among Self-Perception Accuracy, Self-Awareness, Gender, and Leader Effectiveness," *Human Resource Management* 32, nos. 2–3 (1993): 249–63, https://doi.org/10.1002/hrm.3930320205.

22 L. E. Atwater and F. J. Yammarino, "Does Self-Other Agreement on Leadership Perceptions Moderate the Validity of Leadership and Performance Predictions?," *Personnel Psychology* 45, no. 1 (1992): 141–64, https://doi.org/10.1111/j.1744-6570.1992.

tb00848.x.

23 Joan Marques, "Understanding the Strength of Gentleness: Soft-Skilled Leadership on the Rise," *Journal of Business Ethics* 116, no. 1 (2012): 163–71, https://doi.org/10.1007/s10551-012-1471-7.

24 Marques, "Understanding the Strength of Gentleness," 7.

25 [[to come]]

26 Church, "Managerial Self-Awareness."

27 Kristen L. Cullen, William A. Gentry, and Francis J. Yammarino, "Biased Self-Perception Tendencies: Self-Enhancement/Self-Diminishment and Leader Derailment in Individualistic and Collectivistic Cultures," *Applied Psychology* 64, no. 1 (2014): 161–207, https://doi.org/10.1111/apps.12026.

28 Donald D. Warrick, "Leadership Illusions: Important Implications for Leaders and Training and Coaching Leaders," *Organization Development Review* 51, no. 2 (2019): 6–13, chrome-extension://efaidnbmnnnibpcajpcglclefindmkaj/https://cdn.ymaws.com/www.odnetwork.org/resource/resmgr/odreview/vol51/vol51no2-all_pages.pdf.

29 Cam Caldwell, "Identity, Self-Awareness, and Self-Deception: Ethical Implications for Leaders and Organizations," *Journal of Business Ethics* 90, no. 3 (2009): 393–406, https://doi.org/10.1007/s10551-010-0424-2.

30 Michael Walton, "Enhancing Executive Self-Awareness: Two Approaches for Consideration," *IUP Journal of Soft Skills* 16, no. 2 (2022).

31 International Coaching Federation, "ICF Code of Ethics—International Coaching Federation," CoachingFederation.org, 2020, https://coachingfederation.org/ethics/code-of-ethics.

32 Rebecca J. Jones, Stephen A. Woods, and Yves R. F. Guillaume, "The Effectiveness of Workplace Coaching: A Meta-Analysis of Learning and Performance Outcomes from Coaching," *Journal of Occupational and Organizational Psychology* 89, no. 2 (2016): 249–77, https://doi.org/10.1111/joop.12119.

33 Aaron De Smet, Bonnie Dowling, Bryan Hancock, and Bill

Schaninger, "The Great Attrition Is Making Hiring Harder. Are You Searching the Right Talent Pools?," *McKinsey Quarterly,* July 13, 2022, https://www.mckinsey.com/capabilities/people-and-organizational-performance/our-insights/the-great-attrition-is-making-hiring-harder-are-you-searching-the-right-talent-pools.

34 Diane Coutu and Carol Kauffman, "What Can Coaches Do for You," *Harvard Business Review Magazine,* January 2009, https://hbr.org/2009/01/what-can-coaches-do-for-you.

35 Anna Sutton and Cecile Crobach, "Improving Self-Awareness and Engagement Through Group Coaching," *International Journal of Evidence Based Coaching and Mentoring* 20, no. 1 (2022): 35–41, DOI: 10.24384/dqtf-9x16.

36 Remus Ilies, Frederick P. Morgeson, and Jennifer D. Nahrgang, "Authentic Leadership and Eudaemonic Well-Being: Understanding Leader–Follower Outcomes," *The Leadership Quarterly* 16, no. 3 (2005): 373–94, https://doi.org/10.1016/j.leaqua.2005.03.002.

37 Rachel M. Randall, Louis Kwong, Thomas Kuivila, Brett Levine, and Monica Kogan, "Building Physicians with Self-Awareness," *Physician Leadership* 4, no. 3 (2017): 40–44, https://www.physicianleaders.org/articles/building-physicians-with-self-awareness.

38 Amanuel G. Tekleab, Henry P. Sims, Seokhwa Yun, Paul E. Tesluk, and Jonathan Cox, "Are We on the Same Page? Effects of Self-Awareness of Empowering and Transformational Leadership," *Journal of Leadership & Organizational Studies* 14, no. 3 (2007): 185–201, https://doi.org/10.1177/1071791907311069.

39 Malcolm Higgs and Deborah Rowland, "Emperors with Clothes On: The Role of Self-Awareness in Developing Effective Change Leadership," *Journal of Change Management* 10, no. 4 (2010): 369–85, https://doi.org/10.1080/14697017.2010.516483.

40 Ngaio Crook, Ozan Nadir Alakavuklar, and Ralph Bathurst, "Leader, 'Know Yourself': Bringing Back Self-Awareness, Trust and Feedback with a Theory O Perspective," *Journal of Organizational Change Management* (2020), https://doi.org/10.1108/jocm-05-

2020-0131.

41 Church, "Managerial Self-Awareness."

42 Eurich, *Insight*.

43 Jacob Werksman, host, *The Victory Podcast*, episode 17, "Jessica Buchanan: Hostage Survivor Rescued by SEAL Team 6," July 3, 2020, https://www.victory-strategies.com/podcast.

44 Hostage US, Resources, https://hostageus.org/resources/all-resources/.

45 Attributed to Andrew S. Grove in William J. Baumol et al., *Good Capitalism, Bad Capitalism, and the Economics of Growth* (Yale University Press, 2007), 228.